P9-ARK-728

TANGIBLE EVIDENCE THAT
JESUS ROSE FROM THE DEAD

RESURRECTED

Shroud's message revealed
2000 years later

TANGIBLE EVIDENCE THAT
JESUS ROSE FROM THE DEAD

RESURRECTED

Shroud's message revealed
2000 years later

Gilbert R. Lavoie, M.D.

ThomasMore®
– *An RCL Company* –
Allen, Texas

CREDITS
Photos used within text are used with permission and copyright protection of
Holy Shroud Guild, Esopus, N.Y.; copyright 1978, Vernon Miller; and
Gilbert Lavoie.

Holy Shroud Guild: pages 18; 19; 20; 21; 22; 23; 27; 28; 29; 30; 31; 40;
86, 88; 106, Figures 6, 7; 111; 128, Figure 1; 129, Figure 1; 130, Figure
4; 131; 133, Figures 11A, 11B; 136; 137; 165

Vernon Miller: pages cover; 17; 36; 55; 57; 58; 60, back cover

Gilbert Lavoie: pages 89, 90; 91; 99; 101; 102; 103; 104; 106, Figure 8;
113; 114; 116; 118; 128, Figure 2; 129, Figure 3; 130, Figure 5; 132;
133, Figures 9, 10; 134

All scriptural quotations in text, unless otherwise noted, are from the *New
Oxford Annotated Bible,* copyright 1991.

Quotes from the *Jerusalem Bible,* copyright 1966 by Darton, Longman &
Todd, Ltd., and Doubleday and Company, Inc., are found on pages: 104,
105.

Copyright 2000 Gilbert R. Lavoie

All rights reserved. No part of this book shall be reproduced or transmitted in
any form or by any means, electronic or mechanical, including photocopying,
recording, or by any information or retrieval system, without written permission from Thomas More.

Video on the shroud available from Thomas More®:
Product # 7907   ISBN 0–88347–907–9

Send all inquiries to:

Thomas More®
An RCL Company
200 East Bethany Drive
Allen, Texas 75002-3804

Toll Free: 800–264–0368
Fax: 800–688–8356

Printed in the United States of America

ISBN 0–88347–458-1

1 2 3 4 5   04 03 02 01 00

Contents

Foreword

by Gary Habermas

You are about to have a new and unusual experience as you explore a modern look at the resurrection of Jesus. You will not only read, but visually and tangibly participate in this bold attempt to understand the enigma that has fascinated the world for the past two thousand years.

Dr. Lavoie has made a twenty-year study of the only object on earth that may give us some of the very same experiences that the Doubting Thomas experienced in a locked house almost 2,000 years ago. The object of Dr. Lavoie's study is the controversial Shroud of Turin. The Shroud of Turin? Again? I thought that subject was laid to rest years ago after the carbon dating!

If this is your view, then you are in for a surprise. What if this is not the case of faith vs. science? What if science is really the major ally here? Would you be willing to give this odd twist a chance?

And who says that religious people cannot be skeptical? Like Doubting Thomas, some of the best questions are asked by those who have some faith but who also need a little push—or a big one.

Let's go a step further. Perhaps you do not think you are religious at all. Could it possibly be that, far from some dusty artifact, the Shroud of Turin has the potential to point in the direction of answers to some of your deepest questions about life?

You may never know unless you turn a few more pages of this book and see what it is all about. Put on your skeptical glasses if you like. Find a quiet spot where no one will disturb you for three or four hours and enjoy yourself. It is a fast read.

Let me warn you that the author is a man of science. Dr. Lavoie was convinced that the shroud was the real thing until 1988 when he heard the news of the carbon dating results. He did not take the view that the shroud was authentic at all costs. Rather, he assumed that the cloth was a fake, and told his audiences so. But later he changed his mind, convinced that the cumulation of scientific studies more than overwhelmed the carbon dating results. Are you interested in what drove him to this conclusion? He will tell you here.

You can see for yourself the results of some of this scientific testing. Would it surprise you to find that plants placed on this cloth could only have come from the Jerusalem area? Or that they could have been situated there only in the Spring since that is when they bloom? Or that pollens show that the cloth had been in the Middle East before the fourteenth century? Dr. Lavoie explains that nothing keeps the cloth from having a first century origin. You can also pursue the story behind some of the enigmatic blood stains that provide clues concerning how the crucified man was buried.

But Dr. Lavoie goes even further. He argues that the creation of the shroud image defies our ordinary understanding of space and time. He produces some new data which will enable you to experience tangible evidence so as to better understand this claim.

If you have considered that the events of Jesus' resurrection are an illusion, or simply considered it a feverish idea in the minds of the disciples, Dr. Lavoie wrote this book for you. For those who think we enter the third millennium with Jesus as a wise man who preached love and peace but for whom the resurrection is not central to his message of hope, you need to grapple with his arguments. Immerse yourself in these pages and consider how Doubting Thomas might have responded to what you are about to read. Enjoy the experience.

—Gary Habermas, Ph.D., D.D., Chairman of the Department of Philosophy and Theology, Liberty University, Lynchburg, Virginia.

Dedicated to my mother, my wife,
and my children

A Physician's Perspective

Chapter One

How did a carpenter become the central figure of Western civilization? What did this man Jesus do to have the largest following on earth—two billion people—2,000 years after his birth? Why did his life start a revolution that eventually changed a world where people lived in slavery and where women had no power over their lives, into the world of today, where the dignity of all individuals has become the ideal? What event brought this Jesus to center stage at the birth of Western civilization and kept him there for 2,000 years?

Simply stated, it was his resurrection. But it is currently in fashion to write as the real story of the millennium that Jesus' message of love, faith and hope is the reason for his success. It seems it is easier to talk about the man Jesus, the philosopher who imparted great wisdom to the world and avoid mentioning the resurrection, the reason why Christianity survived into the third millennium.

Today some of the followers and even a subset of theologians say that he was a wonderful philosopher and preacher, but they go on to say that his resurrection was not a factual and historic event; it was only in the minds of his disciples. In other words, the resurrection was just an emotional and spiritual event. In light of the current scientific age, everything is supposed to have a natural explanation and if it does not, it never happened. So the resurrection never happened. There is nothing new about this attitude. Doubt about the resurrection has existed from the very beginning. We meet the classic doubter, Thomas the apostle, who demanded scientific proof of the resurrection from the first days after Jesus' death: "Unless I see the marks of the nails in his hands and put my finger in the marks of the nails and my hand in his side, I will not believe." (John 20:25) Thomas not only wanted to see but wanted to touch the areas that would confirm what he saw. For those with a scientific mind that require more than just seeing, we have this Thomas report. After all, the resurrection needed as much confirmation for those of the ancient world as it does in our modern world. The resurrection, if you believe it happened, was no ordinary event; it needed witnesses and witnesses it had.[1]

For those who believe the testimony of the disciples and do not need the physical experience that Thomas required, you are among "those who have not seen and yet have come to believe" and are not looking for further confirmation. However, if God left something more behind should you not be interested? For those who simply want to deepen their faith or for those seeking proof of the resurrection and want more than Thomas' hands-on testimony, you will not be disappointed when you join in my search.

Other than the evidence of the written reports of witnesses, is there anything on this earth that will give us some of the very same insights and experiences that Thomas and his friends had some 2,000 years ago?

Yes there is. It is the Shroud of Turin, a cloth that carries the body image of a man who was crucified in the same way that Jesus was. There has been much said about the cloth, but I can tell you that most of what you'll read about and see in this book is new information that took over twenty years of study to understand. Instruments of measure, chemical tests, and carbon dating are all important, but if you have a scientific mind like Thomas, you will want to see and feel for yourself what this cloth is about. You will participate in the same experience that Thomas had but from a slightly different perspective. Like Thomas who wanted physical proof, if you pay close attention to details, you may see that the image of the man of the shroud was not a painting, that it was not made by human hands. You will learn about how the Jewish people buried their dead at the time of Jesus, and you will discover the significance of the blood that was left on this cloth. If you are a careful reader and pay special attention to the photographs you will see what forensic scientists see, and you will come to know that a crucified man was laid out on this cloth. Moreover, the event of image formation may bring you to contemplate a situation that to this day remains undefined even in the mind of Stephen Hawking, a well-known theoretical physicist at the University of Cambridge. Do you believe that there is anything that exists beyond our understanding of the physical world? You will participate in a simple hands-on experiment and indeed discover a situation that cannot be defined by our ordinary understanding of space and time—not of this world. If you are a careful observer you may even see the image of the man of the shroud raised up from his burial cloth. Even Thomas would likely be moved by these findings for they are all things that he could see, feel and even reproduce for himself if he were here today.

Join me on this unique adventure and as this work draws to its conclusion, I promise to involve in our discussion one of the world's greatest skeptics, Thomas the Doubter. He would demand that the evidence be something that he could see and touch. He would want reproducible proof. As we end our discussion you may even come to ask yourself whether or not the creator of this image was God who left this shroud for people to gaze upon, contemplate and do what only humans can do—wonder. If nothing else you will come to find that it is not simply the wisdom of Jesus that carried him to the third millennium, but rather it was his resurrection.

As you read, I ask that you also demand what Thomas demanded: physical evidence that you can see and touch. Throughout your study you must be as demanding as Thomas and expect to have what is necessary to know whether the image on this cloth was caused by the hand of a man, whether it was a natural phenomenon or a wonder that remains unexplained. Scrutinize the details, for they were hard to come by and they alone tell the story.

Let us begin, but for you to fully understand we have to begin at the place from which I started. And remember, I started this venture many years ago without you, but now I ask you to participate with me in the search.

It was in the spring of 1961, during my first year of college, when I entered an old bookstore in Boston's Scollay Square. Today that bookstore is gone and Scollay Square is now the location of Boston's Government Center. However, the event that occurred on that day was the beginning of an adventure in understanding that continues to move my very being. There at the back of the store was a brown paperback book called *A Doctor at Calvary* by Dr. Pierre Barbet,[2] a French surgeon. As I was a pre-med student at the time, the title word *Doctor* caught my attention.

I thought that I had purchased a physician's retrospective analysis of the crucifixion of Jesus of Nazareth, but as I began to read Barbet's book, I found that he was dealing with an entirely different subject. His work centered on a cloth that displayed the blood-marked image of a naked man. This linen cloth, approximately three and a half by fourteen feet, is known as the Shroud of Turin.

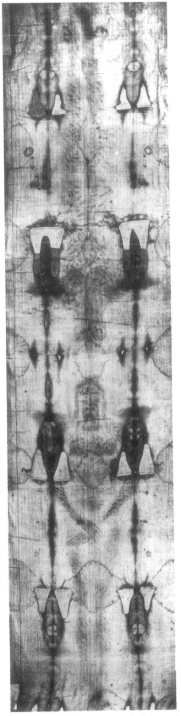

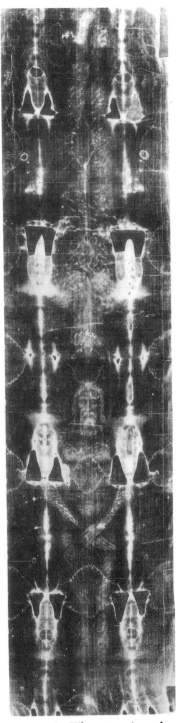

Figure 1A: The actual shroud is a negative image

Figure 2A: The negative plate is a positive image

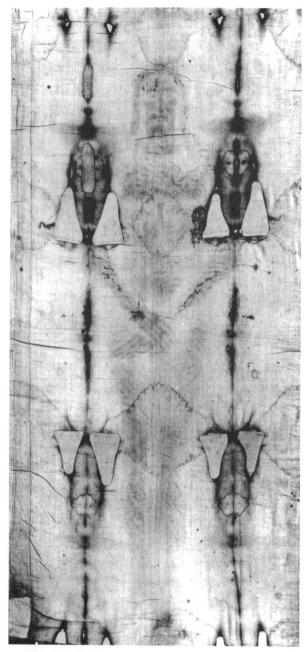

Figure 1B: Front image, negative image

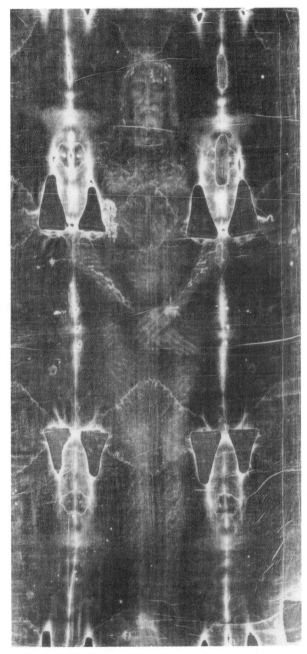

Figure 2B: Front image, positive image

GILBERT R. LAVOIE, M.D.

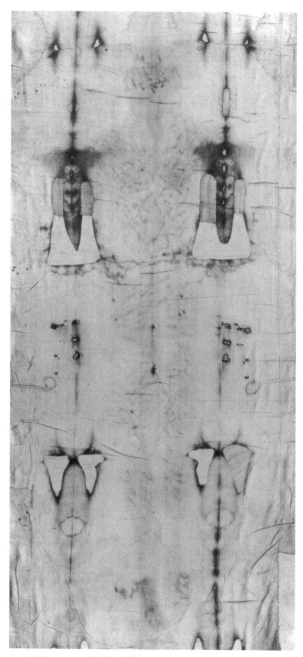

Figure 1C: Back image, negative image

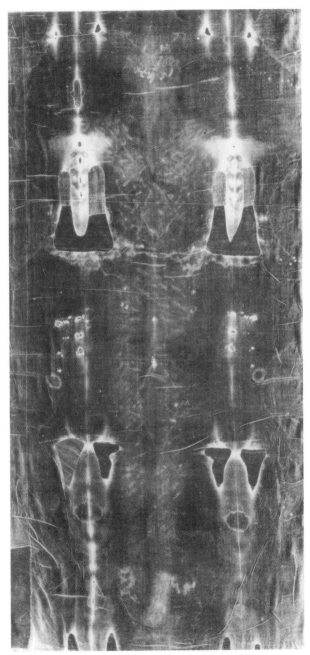

Figure 2C: Back image, positive image

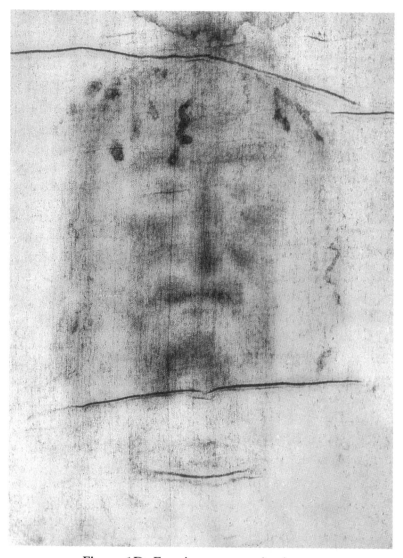

Figure 1D: Face image, negative image

Figure 2D: Face image, positive image

As I continued to read, I found that this shroud has been kept at Turin Cathedral, Italy, since 1578. It was first introduced into western European history in the 1350s at Lirey, France, by a French knight, Geoffrey de Charny, who never revealed the circumstances of how he obtained this cloth. In 1453, the de Charny family transferred the shroud to the House of Savoy, who owned it into the 20th century.[3] While in the hands of the Savoys, the shroud was first kept in Chambery, France, before it was finally brought to Turin in 1578. However, more interesting than its recent history is that from the time of its introduction into Lirey, France, a controversy has raged as to whether or not this shroud image is the work of a 14th-century artist.[4]

What stimulated Barbet's interest in this cloth was the full-scale image of the back and front of a man's body. Most important to the surgeon, Barbet, were the blood marks that accompanied this image. These blood marks suggested that the body of a crucified man had been placed in the supine position on one end of the shroud and then covered by the other end of this long cloth (Figure 1—A, B, C, and D). Barbet, along with a number of other students of this linen, believed that it was the burial shroud of Jesus.

What intrigued these men and what hooked me into the pursuit of this study was that there was something very unusual about the photographs of this cloth. Barbet studied the official photos of the shroud taken in 1931, which are known as the Enrie photographs. However, as I later learned, the first official photographs of the shroud were taken in 1898 by Secondo Pia, an Italian lawyer and amateur photographer. It was during the development of Pia's photographs, in the quiet of his darkroom, that he saw something on his negative plate that not only astounded him, but changed forever the understanding of the shroud image. The image on the photographic negative plate was not the negative image that he expected. (It was not like a negative that you get with a photograph.) Rather the negative plate showed the positive image of a man. (It looked like a photograph that you get with a negative.) (See Figure 2—A, B, C, and D.) Realizing that his negative plate held the positive image of a man brought him to another realization: the shroud image is a negative (Figure 1—A, B, C, and D).[5] How and why would a 14th-century artist paint a negative image?

Dr. Barbet had his first direct experience with the shroud during the Turin exposition in 1933. He was on the steps of the cathedral, and with the help of the light of day, he saw the following:

> . . . from a distance of less than a yard, and I suddenly experienced one of the most powerful emotions of my life. For, without expecting it, I saw that all the images of the wounds were of a colour quite different from that of the rest of the body; and this colour was that of dried blood which had sunk into the stuff. There was thus more than the brown stains on the shroud reproducing the outline of a corpse.
>
> The blood itself had coloured the stuff by direct contact, and that is why the images of the wounds are positive while all of the rest is negative.[6]

After reading this, I looked again at the photographs, and it was true. The blood was positive on the cloth while the image was negative (Figure 1—A, B, C, and D). In contrast, the blood was negative on the photographic negative of the cloth while the image was positive (Figure 2—A, B, C, and D). This meant that the blood marks were photographically opposite to the image that they accompanied. What pictures carry with them photographic opposites? Other than the shroud, I knew of none.

According to Barbet's eyewitness report, the blood marks were encrusted and intertwined with the fibers of the cloth. As per Barbet, "The blood itself had coloured the stuff by direct contact."[7] It was his experience with wounds and bandages as a surgeon that led him to conclude that the blood marks on the shroud were not what people had been casually calling blood flows, but were actual imprints of blood clots on cloth.

After blood flows from a wound, the blood coagulates and becomes a red, jellylike, moist clot that adheres to skin. A slip of the razor or a careless move with a kitchen knife has caused all of us to experience a bleed that turned into a clot. Barbet recognized that the bloodstains on the shroud were the results of cloth coming into contact with clotted blood. He recognized this as easily as I would recognize the transfer of ink to paper caused by the stamp of a postmaster.

In contrast to the blood marks, the fibers of the image of the man were devoid of anything but the brownish fibers themselves. In the words of Barbet:

> There is not a trace of painting to be seen, even in Enrie's highly enlarged direct photographs. (To make this clear, one should explain that this is not just a matter of enlarging a photograph, but of an apparatus which produces on the plate an image enlarged seven times, such as a magnifying glass of the same power would supply to the eye.)[8]

Unfortunately, Barbet did not include Enrie's magnified picture in his book. In order to begin to grasp what caused the image, I had to depend on Barbet's powers of observation and his ability to describe what he saw. All that I knew was that he had not seen paint, but only the "brown stains"[9] that made up the image. I did not understand what those "brown stains" were, but neither did he.

As I turned the pages of Barbet's book, I began to see the subtle details of the image and the blood marks in a way that I

---

* When speaking of right and left, Barbet is referring to the right and left of the man he believes had been under the cloth.

would never have anticipated without his medical insights. His observations of the face, especially the swelling under the right* eye, caused me to stop and pay closer attention to the details (Figures 1D and 2D). At first I did not see the swelling, but after comparing the area under the left eye with that of the right, I could see what Barbet was referring to. It was as if the man had been struck in the face with a fist or a stick at the area of the cheekbone.[10]

Just as revealing as his observations of the face was his study of the scourge marks. These wounds are all over the body but are best seen on the back image (Figures 1C and 2C). The wounds are in pairs and are dumbbell in shape (Figure 3). In Barbet's words: "The two circles represent the balls of lead, while the line joining them is the mark of the thong."[11] Barbet found that most of these wounds are in parallel pairs. From this observation, Barbet deduced that the instrument of scourging had two thongs. Incredibly, these marks appear to correspond to the design of a first-century Roman flagrum. The flagrum was made of a handle from which extended two or more long leather straps that held bone or lead on their ends. The bone or lead ends were dumbbell in shape and were designed to pick out the flesh from the victim.

But there was more. Barbet had come to understand something that was even more telling than the details of the individual scourge marks. His interpretation of the location of these scourge marks on the body image caught my attention. After reading his description, I was able to confirm their position. The stripes on

Figure 3

Pair of dumbbell scourge marks and flagrum

Figure 4

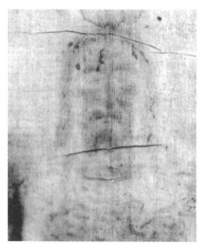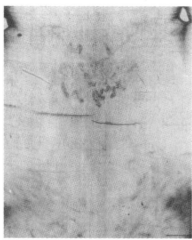

| Blood marks
at the face and hair | Blood marks
at the back of the head |

the back image are oblique, slanting upward toward the right and left shoulders (Figures 1C and 2C). On the buttocks, they change position and are no longer oblique; they are horizontal. On the legs, they are again oblique, slanting downward toward the left. Like Barbet, I contemplated these scourge marks, and I envisioned two floggers, one on each side, standing slightly behind the victim.[12] They would have alternately flogged their victim at shoulder height, causing the oblique stripes of the back. Then they would have struck at waist level, causing the horizontal stripes of the lower backside. Finally, the soldiers would have taken downward swings toward the legs, causing the lower oblique leg wounds. Each strike of small bones on flesh would tear the skin, and blood would flow. Later, these open wounds would ooze clear body fluid like the scraped knees of my boyhood. These injuries would remain moist for hours and eventually allow for the transfer of their paired shapes from body to cloth. There are over one hundred of these marks on the man of the shroud.

Figure 5   Figure 6

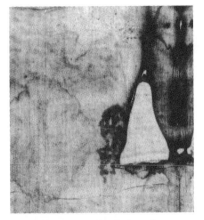   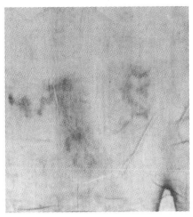

Side wound of the chest   Blood marks of the feet

Barbet made a study of all the major blood marks seen on the shroud. He discussed the cap of thorns causing the blood flows at the back of the head, face, and hair (Figure 4).[13] He then discussed the side wound of the chest and gave his medical interpretation of the blood flow seen at this wound (Figure 5).[14] By simple observation, I could see that these blood flows followed the force of gravity if one assumed that the body of the man of the shroud had been in the vertical position of crucifixion. Barbet also described the blood marks of the feet, which are slightly crossed. Most interesting, however, were his details of the impression in blood made by the sole of the right foot (Figure 6).[15] Finally, he discussed the horizontal blood flow at the small of the back (Figure 7). This blood flow would have meant little to me without his interpretation. According to Barbet, this blood flow occurred after the man was taken from the vertical position of crucifixion and placed in the horizontal position in preparation for burial.[16]

All these studies interested me, but there was one that did much more than that. It was his work on the left wrist and hand that

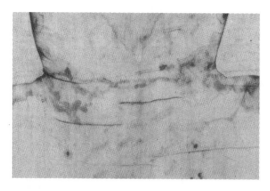

Figure 7

Blood flow
at the small
of the back

remained with me over the years. Even today I marvel at the insights that it brings to the understanding of the shroud (Figure 8). Barbet reasoned that the blood flow of the wrist flowed vertically, "following the laws of gravity."[17] From the vertical flow of this blood mark, he calculated the position of the forearm to be sixty-five degrees from the vertical. In more simple terms, the graphics of this blood mark confirm that the forearm of the man of the shroud had previously been in the position of crucifixion (Figure 9).

Furthermore, for centuries people believed that those crucified had nails placed through the palms of their hands when being secured to the cross. Prior to the 15th and 16th centuries almost all art forms placed the nails through the palms of the hands.[18] Using cadavers, Barbet demonstrated that the weight of a man cannot be held up if the nails are

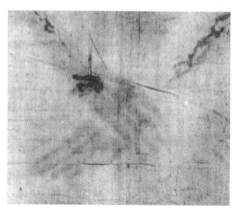

Figure 8

Image
of the hands
and blood flow
at the wrist

Figure 9

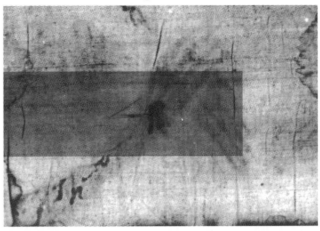

**Image of the left wrist in the position of crucifixion;
shadowed area simulates the crossbeam**

placed through the palms of the hands. Because of the weight
of the body, the nails tear through the flesh and the ligamentous structures of the hands. Barbet demonstrated that to
hold a body in the position of crucifixion the nails had to be
placed through the bony and ligamentous structures of the
wrists. Therefore, the shroud image, with its wrist wound, is
anatomically correct.[19]

Intrigued by the wrist wound, Barbet went on to do another
experiment. In his own words:

> *But these experiments had yet another surprise in
> store for me. I have stressed the point that I was
> operating on hands which still had life in them
> immediately after the amputation of the arm. Now,
> I observed on the first occasion, and regularly from
> then onwards, that at the moment when the nail
> went through the soft anterior parts [of the wrist],
> the palm being upwards, the thumb would bend
> sharply and would be exactly facing the palm by the*

contraction of the thenar muscles, while the four fingers bent very slightly.[20]

The contraction of these thenar muscles, which were still living like their motor nerve, could easily be explained by the mechanical stimulation of the median nerve. . . . And that is why, on the shroud, the two hands when seen from behind only show four fingers and why the two thumbs are hidden in the palms. Could a forger have imagined this?[21]

I looked at the hands of the shroud (Figure 8) and saw for myself that there were no thumbs.

As I finished Barbet's book, his question—"Could a forger have imagined this?"—kept coming back to me. The logical approach that Barbet took, bringing to light the details of the blood marks, the facial beating, the scourging, the crucifixion, and the previously unanswered reason for hands without thumbs, held my attention. Barbet himself did not know the reason for hands without thumbs until he plunged a nail through the wrist of a freshly amputated arm. How could a 14th-century artist have been so anatomically precise, and moreover, why would he attempt to be so precise? Was the artist anticipating the scrutiny of a 20th-century surgeon? Furthermore, this artist would have had to create a negative image five hundred years before the invention of the camera. Then he would have had to put the image on cloth without the use of paint. For me, it seemed that the technology attributed to a forger reached far beyond the realm of genius. At the time, from the perspective of a first-year college student, I felt that Barbet had presented convincing medical evidence demonstrating that this cloth once held the body of a man that had been both scourged and crucified. His book left me wanting to know more. I believe that Thomas would also want to know more.

BECOMING PARTICIPANTS

Chapter Two

ב

In 1978, while reading the *Boston Globe,* I found myself looking at a familiar face that stirred an old memory. Within a moment it all came back to me as clear as it had been on the day that I turned the last page of Barbet's book. I read the newspaper article that accompanied the picture and found that the Shroud of Turin was to be exhibited in Turin, Italy, in the late summer and early fall of 1978.

In late September, 1978, my wife, Bonnie, and I arrived in Turin. We had one purpose in mind: to learn as much as we could about the shroud. However, as our plane landed, I knew that we had no more assurance of succeeding in our venture than would a tourist. In truth, we were outsiders. Furthermore, we were no more experienced regarding the shroud than would be any intent reader of Barbet's book. We were looking for answers, but we did not even know the right questions.

After registering at our hotel, we went directly to Turin Cathedral where the shroud was being displayed. We were not alone. In front of us was a line that stretched around a city block. Three million people had come to Turin over those forty days of the exhibition to see the cloth. After waiting three hours, we finally entered the cathedral and could see, displayed by bright

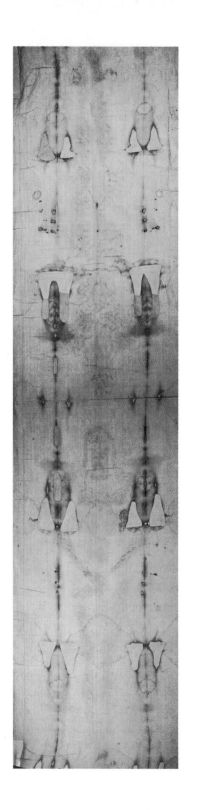

Figure 1

The Shroud of Turin

lights and under bulletproof glass, the linen cloth that had brought us to Europe. Gradually we made our way up toward the front of the church to about 25 feet away from the cloth. From that position, we could easily see the burn marks and repair patches that parallel the faint yellow-brown image of the front and back of a man (Figure 1). The burn marks were the result of a fire that took place in 1532 at the Holy Chapel of Chambery, in France, where the cloth had been previously preserved. The fire caused some of the silver chest to melt, and molten metal burned through the folded cloth that lay within. The melted silver caused the parallel burn marks that enclose the body image of the cloth. Water was used to douse the flames, saving the cloth, but leaving water rings all along the image area of the cloth (Figure 1).[1] As I looked at the cloth, I found that I was close enough to compare the image marks to the blood marks. I could see that the blood was a dark brownish-red color as opposed to the lighter fragile yellow-brown color of the image. At least at first glance, it looked as if Barbet had reported it as it was.

Prior to leaving for Italy, I had tried to contact Reverend Peter Rinaldi, a priest from Port Chester, New York, who was an active organizer of the current shroud exhibition. Unfortunately, I never reached him; he had already left for Turin. However, I did get his Turin address and wrote to him but never received a reply. In Turin, I found that I had misplaced Father Rinaldi's address. Still determined, Bonnie and I began to search for him on the day following our arrival. Fortunately, I had the name of the hotel where the American scientists who had come to study the shroud were staying. We decided to begin our search for our contact at that hotel. I felt very anxious as we walked along the Via Carlo Alberto where the hotel was located, knowing that we were on an uncertain mission, attempting a rendezvous that depended totally on chance.

As we entered Hotel Sitea, we saw several men sitting in one of the alcoves off the lobby. Among them was a white-haired priest. A little embarrassed, we decided that our best strategy was to wait. When the men began to leave, we approached the priest whom we hoped would be Father Rinaldi. I spoke, "Father Rinaldi?" "Yes," he responded. I introduced myself and Bonnie. In a most welcoming tone he said: "My dear Dr. Lavoie, I am so glad to see you!" We were both surprised and moved by his warmth. He acknowledged that he had received my letter. After a short interchange, he assured us of an introduction to some of the members of the American scientific team that had come to study the shroud. He also promised us an opportunity to take close-up pictures of the shroud inside the cathedral. Finally, he gave me one of the last available tickets to the 1978 International Congress on the Shroud of Turin that was to be held the following week. Because of Father Rinaldi's hospitality, we were no longer tourists. Within those few minutes, we became participants in the principal events surrounding the last days of the shroud's exhibition of 1978. Years later I asked him why he treated us with such enthusiasm. His answer, "It was your persistence."

The next day we attempted to learn as much as we could about the shroud. We were told about a small museum dedicated to the history of the shroud on Via San Domenico, not too far from the cathedral. As we entered the museum, Secondo Pia's camera took center stage. It was a large square camera made of wood and was well over two feet in all dimensions. As I looked at it, I realized how large Pia's negative plates had to have been. Because of their size, I had never paid much attention to the small negatives that always accompanied my own photos. However, with Pia's camera in front of me, I could appreciate how he could readily see the details of the positive image of the man of the shroud as it developed on his large negative plate.

Turning from Pia's camera, I began looking along the walls of the small museum. There hung 15th- and 16th-century artistic reproductions of the shroud. These handmade copies demonstrated little similarity to the actual shroud image; they were almost childlike in design. Next, I came to a glass counter. Staring back at me through the glass was the distorted image of a face imprinted on cloth. On further observation I could see that the nose and cheeks of the image were flattened, accounting for much of the distortion. Under the visage was the name Vignon. I recalled Vignon and his theory of image formation in Barbet's book. The masklike face had been produced by placing aloes on a linen, which was then placed over a face prepared with ammonia. The theory was that the ammonia would be derived from the decomposition of body urea (formed by sweat and blood). Barbet, however, felt that Vignon's theory was unsound and even Vignon himself lost confidence in it as the years passed.[2] Nevertheless, I was quite excited about my find and felt that I might be getting closer to understanding the cause of the image. Even as I stood there, I knew that there was a difference between the face on the shroud and the grotesque face behind the glass, but I did not know what caused the difference.

Bonnie and I were intently studying the face when a short round-faced, blue-eyed priest holding a black homburg and displaying a broad smile approached us. "Fellow Americans, I take it," he said, extending his hand to me. It was Reverend Joseph Donovan; we soon became friends. During that trip, Father Donovan bought life-size photographic negative and positive images of the shroud that I later used in my own studies of the cloth. Without his photographs, my story might not have happened.

After we exchanged a few words, Father Donovan invited us to join him. We followed him to an upstairs office above the museum where he was to meet Father Rinaldi with the intent of getting one of the few remaining tickets to the shroud symposium.

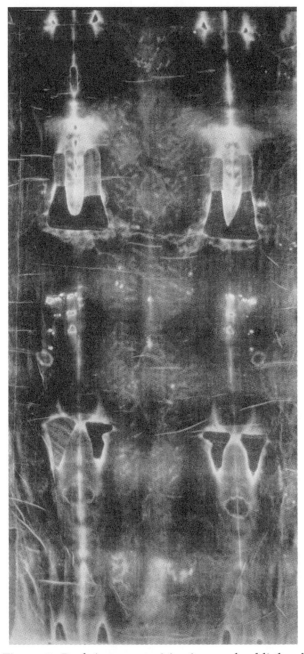

Figure 2: Back image, positive image, backlighted

As we walked into the office, we met Dorothy Crispino, who was also from the United States. She had come to Turin to participate in the organization of the symposium. After the symposium of 1978, Dorothy began to publish a journal, *Shroud Spectrum International,* which gave many the opportunity to have their studies reviewed by others interested in the shroud. Some of the articles that I was able to contribute to her journal became the stepping-stones leading to the completion of this work.

Bonnie took an immediate liking to Dorothy and insisted that she join us for dinner. Before leaving the museum that evening, Dorothy gave us a tour of the small facility. The tour included showing us the life-size positive image of the shroud. The illumination of the shroud image was innovative. The source of light came from behind the photo and shone through the image. While sitting in the darkened room, gazing at the life-size picture of the back image, Dorothy commented, "You know, one thing that this light does is that it brings out the roundness of the muscles, as if the person were right there in front of you." At that moment I agreed, but I did not comprehend the importance of the observation until years later (Figure 2).

On the following day, excited about our discovery and the friends we had made, Bonnie and I decided to head for the Egyptian Museum of Turin. I wanted to confirm that linen cloth could last two thousand years. There we found many fine examples of two-thousand-year-old linens; most were mummy wrappings. Finally, we came across a linen shirt that was in perfect condition, and it was well over two thousand years old. Once I saw that shirt I knew that if linen is kept in a dark, dry place, its longevity is assured.

That night Father Rinaldi called our hotel. He had made arrangements for us to enter the cathedral the next day so that we could take photographs of the shroud. He kept his promise.

Not Made by Human Hands

Chapter Three

Because of the generosity of Reverend Peter Rinaldi, I was now standing on the Piazza San Carlo in front of the Istituto Bancario San Paolo. Inside this structure, the 1978 International Congress on the Shroud of Turin was about to begin. On entering the building, I scanned the conference hall, read through the program, and asked questions, trying to quickly determine who the major players were. Then I let chance do the rest. My first contact was with an older gentleman by the name of Monsieur Antoine Legrand, a man who knew Barbet and studied the shroud with him. I remembered that Barbet had referred to Legrand on several occasions in his book. As Legrand spoke to me, I stood there savoring those few moments that linked me to the past, to an old bookstore in Boston, to the man whose work was the cause of my being there.

Later, as I walked along the central aisle of the auditorium toward the back of the grand room, I met one of the speakers, Dr. Max Frei, a professor of criminology from the University of Zurich. He was a biologist who made a specialty of using microscopic techniques in the field of criminology. He had discovered pollen grains on the shroud and thus was able to give it a geographical history. (Pollen grains are fine powdery microspores that take to the air in order to fertilize their own species.) It had been years since I had looked at pollen under a microscope, and my most recent encounter with it was in the form of a fine yellow-green film that covered my car during the warm season of the year. With Frei standing there in the aisle, I took the opportunity to ask him about his presentation. In fluent English he responded: "It took me five years of my own time to do this work." As he spoke, he pointed to his chest with swift, rapid motions. He spoke with a satisfied smile, and I could sense the enthusiasm that he felt for his work.

In 1982, I read his paper. Here are some excerpts from his study:

> *In 1973, together with two other experts, I was invited by the Archbishop of Turin to compare the structure of the Shroud's tissue, as seen on the photographs taken in 1969, with the original structure of the weave itself. I then discovered under my microscope a certain amount of dust between the linen threads.*
>
> *I requested and was given the permission to take samples of this dust by means of adhesive tape. . . .*
>
> *It was a very difficult task to identify the different pollen-grains in the dust collected. First I had to extract them from the sticking-tape and after cleansing they were embedded in glycerin jelly as permanent mountings, so that they could be studied from all sides under the light-microscope. The only true scientific method for identification of pollen-grains is the direct comparison with a mounting in the same medium of ripe pollen collected from a species to which the unknown pollen might belong.*
>
> *The main problem in this procedure is to find out the right varieties for comparison. Fruitful ideas for comparison often originate from the study of books*

and articles with clear pollen pictures. A good help is the microscopical examination of all pollens available from private collections or public herbariums. In the case of the Shroud, all these sources gave only very few positive results. So I was obliged to make systematic studies of pollen-producing plants growing in such countries where the Shroud—supposing it was authentic—might have been contaminated. A positive identification of such pollens would be a confirmation of the Shroud's stay in that particular botanical region, while negative results concerning the whole flora of a country would allow the exclusion of the geographical area in question as source of contamination.[1]

Frei's words, "confirmation of the Shroud's stay in that particular botanical region," caused me to think of the shroud as a cloth that carried its own passport. Instead of the stamp of the customs' official naming the country of entrance, there were the pollens that clung to the cloth allowing Frei to determine its itinerary. Frei's own words best tell us what he discovered:

From 1974 to 1978, I traveled several times (in different floreal seasons) through Palestine, Turkey (especially Anatolia and the region around Constantinople), through Cyprus, France and Italy, collecting pollens for direct comparison under the microscope. I devoted all my spare time to these journeys and the consequent laboratory work. . . .

I succeeded in identifying 57 different plants which have left microscopical evidence on the Shroud. . . . Every identification has been controlled not only under the optical microscope at magnifications

*ranging from 60x to 1200x, but also under the
scanning electron microscope. . . .*

*None of the pollens was glued to the cloth with
tempera or covered with tempera. This is strong
evidence against the possibility of the Shroud's being
a painted fake.*[2]

Frei found desert plants that grow in soils that have a high
concentration of salt. Many of these plants grow around the
Dead Sea and are not found at all in Italy and France. He found
plants of rocky hills that grow in Israel and neighboring
countries. (Two still grow on the walls of ancient Jerusalem.) He
found Mediterranean plants that grow in Israel as well as in
France and Italy. He found plants from Anatolia as well as some
from Constantinople (Istanbul). He found plants that are widely
distributed in central Europe (France and Italy). He found no
plants from Cyprus.[3] Frei concluded that:

*Plants on the Shroud from Palestine and Anatolia
are so numerous, compared to the species from
Europe, that a casual contamination or a pollen-
transport from the Near East by storms in different
seasons cannot be responsible for their presence,
as I have explained in several conferences and
publications. The predominance of these pollens
must be the result of the Shroud's stay in such
countries where these plants form part of the
normal vegetation.*[4]

Frei leaves us with two very interesting pieces of information:
(1) Even though the known history of the shroud is confined to
France and Italy from the 1350s on, with Frei's pollen study we
now know that the shroud did have an earlier Asian and
Holyland history that preceded the 1350s. This history was
either unknown or for some reason never passed on by its first

recorded European owner, Geoffrey de Charny. (2) Frei found no tempera on the pollens of the shroud. This was significant in that he took some of his sticking-tape samples directly from the shroud image in 1973. Frei felt that this was strong evidence against the shroud image being a painting. It also confirmed Barbet's personal observations, as well as his deductions from looking at Enrie's magnified picture of the shroud image, that the shroud image was not a painting.

A new dimension has been added to Frie's study through the work of Alan Whanger, M.D., and his wife Mary. In 1989, while attending a shroud symposium in Paris, the Whangers showed me their observations of very faint images of flora on the non-image areas of the shroud, mainly about the head of the image. They identified 28 species of plants, all found in Israel. In 1995 the Whangers went to Israel seeking the help of Professor Avinoam Danin, an authority on the plant life of Israel, who works at the Alexander Silberman Institute of the Life Sciences at the Hebrew University.

On April 13, 1997, the Department of Media Relations and Publications from the Hebrew University of Jerusalem released a news article and the following excerpts tell the story:

> *Prof. Danin examined their [Whangers'] findings, verified them, and even determined that additional images found on the garment could be associated with plants from the land of Israel. . . . Danin found images of summer and winter leaves of zygophyllum which are characteristic of the plant pollen grains from the rockrose [which] were recovered from the shroud in the 1970s by Dr. Max Frei, a forensic scientific expert from Switzerland. This kind of "double proof" (images and pollen) shows conclusively that there were indeed rockroses that were placed with the shroud, says Prof. Danin.*

Prof. Danin says that his research shows that the types of plants found on the shroud—when compared to his mapping of these same plants as found in nature—show that 70 percent of these species can be found within a 10 x 10 square-kilometer area whose center lies in an area between Jerusalem and Jericho. Prof. Danin noted further that the zygophyllum grows only in Israel, Jordan and Sinai, with its northernmost boundary in the world being at the sea level sign on the highway between Jerusalem and Jericho. In view of this, one can narrow down even further the origin of the shroud and say definitely that one is dealing with the Jerusalem area. The fact that a winter leaf was found on the zygophyllum, together with remnants of the stalk from the preceding year, proves, says Prof. Danin, that it was plucked in the spring, which was the season identified with most of the plants revealed on the shroud.

The Whangers and Professor Danin thus complement Frei's work and present evidence that the shroud originated in the Jerusalem area in the spring of the year which is the time of the Passover. A precedence for using flowers in Jewish burials is found in 2 Chronicles 16:14 (verbal communication with Anthony Opisso, M.D.)

Frei's itinerary of the shroud, as determined by the pollens, also coincided with Ian Wilson's theories as to the whereabouts of the shroud prior to the 1350s. Ian Wilson, a history graduate of Oxford and a journalist, is the author of the book *The Shroud of Turin*, published in 1978. He was also presenting at the conference, which gave me the opportunity to hear about his work firsthand. His book is a compilation of fragmented historical reports that tell of an image-bearing linen cloth that carried the likeness of Jesus. He begins his story in the early part of the first century and takes us from Jerusalem to the ancient city of Edessa, now called Urfa, located in the southeastern part of Turkey. There, an image-bearing cloth was given to the incumbent king, Abgar, where it remained hidden for five centuries. It resurfaced at the same site in A.D. 544 as "the divinely made image not made by the hands of man"[5] as it was reported by the Syrian historian Evagrius (527–600). Regarding the image, Wilson quotes Edward Gibbon's *The Decline and Fall of the Roman Empire*:

> *Before the end of the sixth century these images made without hands . . . were propagated in the camps and cities of the Eastern empire; they were the objects of worship and the instruments of miracles; and in the hour of danger or tumult their venerable presence could revive the hope, rekindle the courage, or repress the fury of the Roman legions. Of these pictures the far greater part, the transcripts of a human pencil, could only pretend to a secondary likeness and improper title; but there were some of higher descent, who derived their resemblance from an immediate contact with the original. . . . The most ambitious aspired from a filial to a fraternal relation with the image of Edessa.[6]*

In A.D. 944, the image of Edessa, also known as the Mandylion, which Wilson believes to be the shroud, arrived in Constantinople where it remained for over 250 years. Wilson's theory is interesting, but he has to contend with the fact that the Mandylion was thought to have been a facial image whereas the shroud displays a total body image. In 1998, Wilson documents new evidence to back his theory. He writes:

(August 16, 1944). The cloth [of Edessa] is carried around the walls of Constantinople in its casket, then taken to Hagia Sophia, where it is placed on the "throne of mercy." On this occasion, Gregory, archdeacon of Hagia Sophia, delivers a sermon in which he imparts that it bears not only "the drops of sweat from the agony [in Gethsemane] which flowed from [Christ's] face like drops of blood but also blood and water [haima kai hudor] from his very side." This indicates (i) that there was more to the imprint on the cloth of Edessa that just a face; and (ii) that the imprint included blood of the Passion and must thereby have been created after Jesus was taken down from the cross, i.e. precisely corresponding to the Turin Shroud.[7]

Wilson's most convincing documentation locates the shroud in Constantinople. From the pages of the diary of a French crusader by the name of Robert de Clari, we find the following account:

There was another of the churches which they called My Lady St. Mary of Blachernae, where was kept the sydoine [shroud cloth] in which Our Lord had been wrapped, which stood up straight every Friday so that the figure of Our Lord could be plainly seen there.[8]

And no one, either Greek or French, ever knew what became of this sydoine after the city was taken.[9]

This was written during the first part of the 1200s after Constantinople was sacked by the army of the Fourth Crusade.[10] Wilson believes, as some other scholars do, that this was the time when the shroud, along with many other treasures of Constantinople, began its long journey to the West. Eventually, the shroud appeared in Lirey, France, in the 1350s.[11] For those interested in further details, Wilson's books in 1978 and 1998 are a good start as a reference.[12]

Wilson continues to gather more evidence connecting the mandylion to the shroud. However, more important than how he resolves the whereabouts of the shroud before it was introduced into western European history by Geoffrey de Charny are the quotes that he uses to build up the evidence for his case. They carry with them a definite common theme. They tell us (1) that in the East there existed a cloth that carried an image of Jesus and (2) that there was something unusual about this image, so unusual that those who described it believed that it was not a painting, that it was not the work of an artist, that it was "not made by the hands of man."

"Not made by the hands of man" hit home when I first read the words. I must admit that after reading Barbet's work, I was moved to want to know more about the shroud image. The driving force that motivated me was the possibility that the shroud image was not made by human hands. It was that lure that brought Bonnie and me to Turin and to the conference that I was attending.

It was years later before I realized that the Bible was very much concerned with this very same concept: things are made either by human hands or by God. From Deuteronomy I read, "There you will serve other gods made by human hands, objects of wood and stone that neither see, nor hear, nor eat, nor smell" (Deuteronomy 4:28). The corollary is well defined in Hebrews: ". . . then through the greater and perfect tent (not made with hands, that is, not of this creation)" (Hebrews 9:11). The biblical meaning is clear: that which is made by human hands is from man and that which is not made by human hands is from God.

After hearing Wilson's presentation, I met with Dr. John Jackson for about thirty seconds as he raced from the auditorium. Jackson, a physicist, was the energy behind the American move to study the shroud. His presentation was one of the highlights of the congress. He placed a photograph of the shroud image under a VP8 image analyzer. This electronic device is ". . . ideally suited for determining whether a given image contains distance information because it converts image shading into relief."[13] Jackson found that the frontal image of the shroud has a three-dimensional quality.[14] Photographs of people do not exhibit this quality. This quality of three dimensionality intrigued a number of scientists who followed this enthusiastic man to Turin. John's drive, along with the efforts of all those who came with him to Turin in 1978, deserves much credit for establishing the American scientific literature that is now available on the shroud. Much later, in 1992, Whanger discovered another quality about the image. He found "X-ray-like images of internal body structures" such as bones of the face and hands.[15] So now this ancient cloth has upon it an image that not only seems to appear as a photographic negative, but also has information allowing it to display under appropriate circumstances a three-dimensional quality as well as an X-ray-likeness that seems to demonstrate bones of the hands and face. This is a unique and complex image that one may say is more than a photograph: it seems to possesses some characteristics of an X-ray and carries with it information that gives it a three-dimensional quality.

When I met Vern Miller in the grand room of the congress, I was excited to learn that I was being introduced to one of the official professional photographers for the American scientific team. However, I had no idea where that initial meeting would eventually lead me. A few years later I met with Miller at a Boston waterfront restaurant. He had with him a folder of shroud slides that he and his team had taken while in Turin in 1978. Miller held his hand out over the table, handing me a slide

Figure 1

Micrograph taken at the image area of the nose
at 64x magnification

that he explained was a micrograph. He explained that it was taken at 64x magnification. It was taken at the image area of the nose, which happens to be the darkest portion of the entire shroud image.

I held the slide to the light, and I could see exactly what caused the image (Figure 1). For me it was the visual confirmation of what Barbet had seen at one yard away in 1933. There was no paint causing the image; anyone could verify this by simply looking at the slide. I could see that the individual fibers of each thread were yellowed. It was these individual yellowed fibers of each thread, not paint, that caused the image. Subsequently, Miller sent me other micrographs. One of them was taken at the blood area of the chest wound at 32x magnification (Figure 2). In and about the fibers is intertwined debris that Barbet had believed to be blood. Included is a final micrograph (Figure 3) for comparison to the blood area. It is also taken at 32x magnification but at the image area of the right eye. Just like the micrograph of the nose image taken at 64x magnification, no debris can be seen here.

With Miller's micrographs in hand, I was convinced that the image was not a painting. I wasn't alone. All of the American scientists who studied the shroud, except one, found that it was not a painting.[16, 17] (The work of one scientist,[18] who believes the shroud to be a painting, was carefully reviewed by the other scientists. After careful evaluation, their conclusion was still the same: the shroud image is not a painting.[19]) However, I did not know what had caused the yellowing of the fibers, and I did not know whether the debris that Barbet believed to be blood was indeed blood. The answers to these two questions—(1) what caused the yellowing of the fibers that caused the image and (2) what was the debris that Barbet believed to be blood—came from a man who did not attend the congress in 1978. Jackson and others had arranged to have some of the sticking-tapes that

Figure 2

Micrograph taken at the blood area of the chest wound
at 32x magnification

Figure 3

Micrograph taken at the image area of the right eye
at 32x magnification

had been placed over the blood marks and image marks of the shroud given to a man by the name of Dr. Alan Adler. Adler, a professor of chemistry from Western Connecticut State University, is an expert on porphyrins, which are organic chemicals that form part of the structure of red blood cells. Adler analyzed the particles and fibers that adhered to the sticking-tapes.

My first encounter with Adler was in his office at Western Connecticut State University in 1982. As I entered his office, he was sitting at his desk surrounded by walls covered with books from floor to ceiling. We began by discussing his work on the red-orange globules that he found on the sticking-tapes that had been placed over the blood areas of the shroud. He told me of the difficulties that he had faced in removing these particles from the tapes in order to prepare them for chemical analysis. He spent a great deal of time explaining his confirmatory tests for blood. First, he visually compared the microscopic examination of the shroud blood area to a control: a 300-year-old linen impregnated with twelve-month-old blood. Under the microscope, the fibers and the crystals of both were similar in physical appearance, except the crystals of his control sample were slightly more garnet colored.[20] After this examination, he eventually "established by detection of heme derivatives, bile pigments, and proteins,"[21] the presence of whole blood on the shroud. (Anyone interested in pursuing the chemistry of Adler's blood studies should refer to his excellent journal articles.[22])

As we went on to the next topic, that of the yellowed fibers that caused the image, Adler stopped and said, "You know, one of the best tests they did during those five days of testing in Turin was one of the simplest tests they did." He went on to explain the visual test that the team members performed. They shone a light through the cloth. As the light passed through the cloth, the blood images could be easily seen, but the body image could not be seen (Figure 4). What did this mean?

Figure 4

 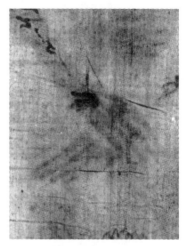

Transmitted light;	Shroud image;
no image seen	normal light

Adler explained that the blood marks were opaque, and because of this, they were poor transmitters of light. In contrast, that which caused the body image was not opaque and was so thin that light went right through it and did not produce an outline of the image as did the blood. This meant that the light went through the image in the same way as it went through the plain cloth. He went on to further support this statement by explaining that the American scientists had removed part of the backing cloth that had been sewn onto the back of the shroud in order to preserve the shroud after the fire of 1532. In doing so, the scientific team discovered that the blood marks had soaked through to the back side of the shroud[23] whereas the image marks were not seen from the back of the cloth.[24]

Adler then explained that a single thread of the shroud cloth was made up of many very small (10 to 15 microns in diameter)[25] linen fibers. The width of one of these fibers is much smaller

than that of a human hair. Only the topmost fibers of the thread
were yellowed. These yellowed fibers, composed of cellulose,
were found only on the image side of the cloth and were responsible for the image. As he spoke, I realized that he was confirming
what I had seen for myself when Vern Miller handed me one of
his micrographs of the image (Figure 1).

After extensive chemical testing, Adler concluded (1) that
there is no paint medium coating the image fibers and (2) that
there are no stains or dyes causing the image. Rather, the
yellowing of the shroud image fibers was produced by a dehydrative oxidative process that affected the fiber (cellulose)
structure itself and caused it to yellow. In other words, this
process is a degradation of the fibers themselves and is identical
to the aging of linen, causing linen to turn from white to yellow.
Adler explained that light, heat, or an acid (such as sulfuric acid)
can all yellow linen fibers like those found in the image area of
the shroud. Therefore, it was not a painted image, but rather, it
was the result of a chemical change of the cellulose itself. (For
those interested in the chemistry of the image fibers of the
shroud, Adler's article is excellent.[26])

Adler went on to explain that even though he understood
the chemistry of the cellulose that makes up the yellowed fibers
of the image, he still did not know what event took place to
cause the image. He leaned back in his chair and went on to say
that with the use of perspiration,[27] the yellowing of the topmost
fibers can be reproduced when linen is placed over the flat
surfaces of a body. However, when it came to more complex
surfaces, such as the face, this contact mechanism is not capable
of causing the image that is seen on the shroud.[28] John Jackson
spent years attempting to reproduce the shroud image without
success. He investigated direct contact, diffusion, radiation from
a body shape or an engraving, dabbing powder on a bas-relief,
electrostatic imaging, and hot bas-relief (a rubbing image), but

none reproduced the image of the shroud.[29] There is presently no known mechanism that can reproduce this body-to-cloth image transfer.[30]

Adler shared with me another piece of information that continues to fascinate me. On removing the blood from the blood-covered fibers, Adler found that these fibers, instead of being yellow as they were at the image areas, were white. What did this mean? Because the fibers under the blood were white, it meant (1) that the blood went onto the cloth before the image marks and (2) that the blood protected the fibers from whatever caused the image. Therefore, the blood came first; the image came later.[31]

I did not meet Dr. Eric Jumper at the congress, but later at the cathedral during a private showing of the shroud. Jumper, in engineering and presently teaching at the University of Notre Dame, spent a great deal of time studying the shroud and published several papers regarding his findings. His best article, "A Comprehensive Examination of the Various Stains and Images on the Shroud of Turin,"[32] is a must-read for the scientifically inclined. I called Jumper to ask him about the observations that he had made concerning the image marks. He explained that their (the scientists') goal was to understand what caused the image. On viewing the shroud image under magnification (Figure 1), he and his colleagues found no excess material around the image fibers. The only place where the fibers were cemented together was at the blood-mark areas. Furthermore, they found that the topmost fibers of the threads of the cloth were yellowed, and it was these yellowed fibers that caused the image.

Jumper followed along the length of the image fibers and found that as the yellowed uppermost fibers dipped down under another thread, they were no longer yellow but remained their original white. Likewise, as the fibers followed a normal twist of the thread, the top fibers were yellowed while the lower part of the fibers remained white. Therefore, whatever caused the image affected only the uppermost fibers, even to the point of not wicking (absorbing and conveying fluid along a fiber like the wick of an oil lamp) along the fiber as a liquid would do if it had been applied to the shroud surface.[33]

As Jumper and his associates teased at the fibers of the threads, they made another observation. They found that whatever caused the yellowing of the shroud fibers penetrated down into each thread the depth of only one fiber. Jumper remembers that after they left the examining room they argued about whether the yellowed fibers penetrated the depth of the thread by one or two fibers. In attempting to decide what was the correct observation, they all went back to their notebooks to see what they had documented. Everyone had made the same observation: the yellowed fibers that caused the image were only one fiber deep.[34, 35]

As I listened to Jumper, I felt that I was being taken right down into the image and fabric of the shroud. I was enjoying every moment of Jumper's firsthand observations. He was someone who had been there; he was an eyewitness, just as Barbet had been in 1933. Jumper went on to say that he later looked carefully at the micrographs taken by Vern Miller and made other observations regarding the image fibers (Figure 1). He saw that there were examples everywhere of yellowed image fibers lying side by side to white non-image fibers. He also noted that the yellowing of the individual fibers was uniform: the amount of yellowing of each fiber was a quantitative event. Each fiber that was yellowed was yellowed to the same extent as the next image fiber. In other words, there was no graduating difference in yellowness of the fibers. Rather, each fiber held almost exactly the same quantity of yellowness.

If every topmost fiber of yellowed threads contained the same shade of yellow, then what caused the difference in the shading of the image? Jumper explained that the difference in the shading of yellow from one area of the image to another was dependent on the number of yellowed fibers present. He made a count of them, and if one area was darker than the other, that area would contain more yellowed fibers.[36] Regarding why we see the changes in shading that causes the image, Jumper's words best describe it: "It's like the dots of newspaper print. If you want to make an area darker, you put in more dots."

There is one thing that is certain: the image is not a painting. Jumper is convinced of this and so is anyone who understands his detailed study of the image fibers and also understands the wicking ability of linen. The liquid medium of a paint would wick along the fibers and color the fibers as they dip below the threads of the weave. Furthermore, a liquid medium would spread adjacently from fiber to fiber, and if enough is added, it would soak through to the opposite side of the cloth. If the paint were more viscous (thick), it would collect on and between the fibers. It would not look like what is seen at the image areas, but would look more like what is seen at the blood areas.

Several years ago, I followed up on a claim that the shroud image is a painting and examined the artist's rendition. First of all, the image was not even the same color as that of the shroud image, but more important, the medium had soaked through to the back side of the cloth. That experience has made me realize the significance of Jumper's very specific description of the image fibers of the shroud. Those who claim that the shroud image is a painting will have to demonstrate that their reproduction matches what Jumper and his associates have described at the fiber level of the cloth. At the same time, they will have to create a negative image. The difficulty of producing the shroud image by hand is best underlined by the words of Dr. Adler:

For a painter to have created this image, he would have needed a paintbrush the size of a fiber which is less than half the width of a human hair.

On the last day of the congress, there came an intense cry for carbon dating; it came from every country represented. In response, it was explained that there was a new carbon-dating technique available to date the shroud, and all one needed was a single ten-inch thread. Ten years later a carbon dating test was done. The *New York Times* carried three articles on October 14, 1988. The first summed it up:

Radiocarbon tests conducted independently by three laboratories this year . . . concluded that the shroud cloth was created between 1260 and 1390.

Each of the labs tested[37] a piece of the shroud cloth that was not much larger than a postage stamp. These small pieces were obtained from a sample cloth that had been cut from one end of the fourteen-foot linen. The first *New York Times* article went on to give two theories: (1) The image was a painting. (This chapter provides the evidence that the image was not a painting.) (2) "Organic residue left on the cloth by some person was discolored by heat and aging to produce a brownish image." (Chapters 5 and 7 provide the evidence that this contact process theory is invalid.)

My initial response to the radiocarbon date is difficult to explain. It is the feeling that one gets when two apparent "truths" collide. Using technical data to make medical decisions has been part of my life. Now, with the carbon-dating information at hand, I made the decision to accept the shroud as a 14th-century cloth. In 1988 I began my presentations by stating that carbon dating had proved that the shroud cloth was from the 14th century, but since that time new information has been forthcoming.

Since 1988 more data has become available regarding the origin of the shroud. Whanger's and Danin's recent work (1997) concludes that there are, on the non-image areas of the shroud, very faint images of spring flora from the Jerusalem area. Frei (1978) had previously discovered on the shroud, pollen grains, some of which come from some of the same type of flora seen on the cloth. The above provides proof that the shroud had a pre-European pre-fourteenth-century history. Whanger's and Danin's study also presents evidence that the shroud originated in the Jerusalem area at the spring of the year—the time of Passover—the time of Easter (see pages 49-50). Furthermore, in 1999, Whanger and Danin examined a cloth that some believe to be the face cloth of Jesus. This cloth is called the Surdarium of Oviedo and is from El Salvador Cathedral of Oviedo, Spain. It can be dated back to the eighth century and has a history which suggests that it goes back to the first century in Jersualem. They discovered that this cloth and the shroud have a blood pattern that is nearly congruent and also have pollens from an identical plant species. From their study they have concluded, "This pollen association, congruence of blood patterning, and probable identical blood type suggests the radiocarbon dating (Damon et al., 1989) of the Shroud to only the Middle Ages as untenable."[38]

New information on radiocarbon dating of the shroud is also available.[39] An excellent 1989 article, "Carbon Dating the Shroud of Turin," explains that the radiocarbon scientists prepared a protocol requiring six samples of the shroud and the use of seven laboratories in order to assure the best result. The reality is that the protocol was abandoned and the scientists, through no fault of their own[40] were given only one sample of the shroud.[41] This sample was portioned and three pieces were then given to three radiocarbon dating labs, each lab receiving one piece of this one sample.

Regarding taking samples from a study object, the carbon dating article further states: "Archaeologists should be sure the samples they take are representative and homogeneous with respect to the questions being asked."[42] In the case of the shroud, the question being asked is the date of origin of the shroud. The importance of this test, which uses samples, is to be certain that the samples reflect the whole. In this case the one sample taken from the shroud should be "representative of" and "homogeneous" with the rest of the cloth. If it isn't, no matter how good the dating test is, there will be a sampling bias which would jeopardize the accuracy of the test. Now, in asking if the one sample taken from the shroud was or was not representative of the rest of the cloth, one has to remember that no other samples were taken from other parts of the cloth. Therefore, there is no basis for comparison to assure that the first and only sample taken is or is not "homogeneous" or "representative" of the rest of the cloth.

To make the problem of taking only one sample perfectly clear, look at sampling from your own perspective by answering the following question: If I take a blood sample from you and make the diagnosis of a particular cancer without even examining you and then treat you without taking any further blood samples to confirm the diagnosis, would you be satisfied with this?

Dr. Alan Adler (1996) has done an examination of a piece of the shroud sample used for radiocarbon dating, comparing it to the non-image area of the cloth by Fourier Transform Infrared microspectrophotometry and by a scanning electron microprobe. The results clearly indicate differences in chemical composition. "The radiocarbon samples are not representative of the non-image sample that comprise the bulk of the cloth."[43] Therefore, the sample given to the radiocarbon scientists does not follow their own criteria that a sample be "representative" and "homogeneous."

In conclusion, the accuracy* of the radiocarbon test results is questionable. Using the appropriate protocol, the radiocarbon test needs to be repeated. So the bottom line is that all the above information indicates that the 1988 radiocarbon dating test results are in error and the shroud could very well be from the first century.

What is interesting about science is that whenever you study a subject, even though you try your hardest to verify something by going back to the original scientific literature as this chapter does, you end up having to trust someone about something. It can almost be compared to listening to the witnesses who saw Jesus after his resurrection. Thomas would have difficulty with some evidence in this chapter except for the micrographs which he could see. If you are a skeptic like Thomas it is only that information that you will accept. Frankly, I had to start from the micrographs before I was convinced that the image is not a painting.

In summary (1) we know from the pollen and faint flower images that the shroud originated from Jerusalem in the spring of the year. (2) Historians traced the shroud to Constantinople in 944 and tell us that there was an ancient cloth that goes back to the first century. This ancient cloth was in the East and is said to have an image of Jesus that was "not made by the hands of man" (3) The image is complex containing not only photographic information but a three-dimensional quality as well as x-ray-like information. (4) Magnified photographs of the image demonstrate no paint, and the yellowness of only the topmost fibers of the threads are responsible for the image. Technology to this date has not been able to reproduce this complex image at the microscopic level. (5) The shading is more like the technology of

* The precision of the radiocarbon dating results done by the three labs is not in question, but it is the accuracy[44] that is in question. For those interested in further discussion, see the three references cited. [45]

newspaper print—"if you want to make an area darker, you put in more dots." (6) What looks like blood has been chemically substantiated to be blood, and the blood came first, the image second. (7) New information indicates that the radiocarbon dating results are in error. The shroud can be historically dated back to the 8th century, and there is no information that tells us that the shroud could not be from the first century.

Now let us consider the above summary. It is convincing information and it points out that the shroud image is complex and that the yellow fibers ("dots") that make up the image are unique like the pixels on the screen of your computer. It is not a painting, and no one to this date has reproduced this complex image. So remember the Thomas rule. If you don't see it, it does not exist. Next time you see a television program on the shroud and they have a qualified artist show you how the shroud was painted, ask yourself the following question: Is that image like the complex image of the shroud, and if you had the micrographs of that artwork, would they look like the micrographs of the shroud image?

When faced with various opinions, adopt a rule of thumb, a scientific rule of thumb. Whatever speculation is made about the cause of the shroud image, whether it be a painting or natural phenomenon, before you believe the theory, this complex image must be reproduced at the microscopic level that is seen on the shroud micrographs. I believe that Thomas would be satisfied with this stipulation.

JEWISH BURIAL CUSTOMS

Chapter Four

How does one begin to study the blood marks on the shroud cloth—blood marks that some claim to be the creation of an artist? It was 1979 when I called Harvard University and asked for the name of a professor who was a specialist in iconography, the study of religious images. I was given the name of Dr. Ernst Kitzinger, who had spent a lifetime studying ancient paintings of Jesus from both the East and the West. I was fortunate to meet with him just before his permanent departure to England where he planned to retire.

I asked Kitzinger the following question: "Can you show me some works of artists who have painted blood marks like the ones that you see on the Shroud of Turin?" His response was: "The Shroud of Turin is unique in art. It doesn't fall into any artistic category. For us, a very small group of experts around the world, we believe that the Shroud of Turin is really the Shroud of Constantinople. You know that the crusaders took many treasures back to Europe during the 13th century, and we believe that the shroud was one of them. As for the blood marks done by artists, there are no paintings that have blood marks like those of the shroud. You are free to look as you please but you won't find any." I did look, and he was right; I have never found any. Nor has anyone else.

If artists had never created blood marks like those of the shroud, then there had to be some explanation as to why the blood marks of the shroud were unique. I decided to go back to the basics and deal with what was at hand—the blood marks of the shroud itself. The only logical option available was to attempt to reproduce the blood marks of the shroud. If Barbet were right and the blood marks were actually transfers of moist clots on a body to cloth, then there should be no problem in reproducing them. However, if I was to pursue this study correctly, I felt obliged to go back into history and find out how the Jews buried their dead at the time of Jesus.

To my surprise, I found that the Jewish burial custom at the time of Jesus was the same as it is today: when a person dies, the body is washed prior to burial.[1,2] Furthermore, this custom was well known, and Christian scholars had assumed for centuries that Jesus' body was washed because "they took the body of Jesus and wrapped it with the spices in linen cloths, according to the burial custom of the Jews" (John 19:40). However, since there are numerous blood marks on the shroud cloth, it is evident that the man covered by the shroud was not washed. If Jesus had been washed according to the Jewish custom, then one would have to conclude that the Shroud of Turin is not the shroud of Jesus.

Believers in the authenticity of the shroud had a different perspective. Over the past 80 years most of the books written by the proponents of the shroud state that the body should have been washed as part of the Jewish tradition, but it wasn't washed because the Sabbath was imminent, and therefore, there was no time to wash the body. That is the information that I had available at the start of my study. However, when Bonnie and I finished our academic pursuit of how the Jews buried their dead at the time of Jesus, I understood the real meaning of John's words "according to the burial custom of the Jews."

John Reagan, a pharmacist in West Roxbury, Massachusetts, where I practiced medicine, said that he would not have any trouble finding out how the Jews used aloes and myrrh in their burial rites. When I entered his pharmacy weeks later, he greeted me with a smile of accomplishment and said, "I couldn't find anything on aloes and myrrh, but I did find that the Jews don't wash the blood from the body of a man who dies a violent death." I was astonished and blurted out, "Where did you find that?" "In Maurice Lamm's book, *The Jewish Way in Death and Mourning.*"

It was just as Reagan said:

> *The blood that flows at the time of death may not be washed away. When there is other blood on the body that flowed during lifetime, from wounds or as a result of an operation, the washing and taharah [purification] are performed in the usual manner.*

> *Where the deceased died instantaneously through violence or accident, and his body and garments are completely spattered with blood, no washing or taharah is performed. The body is placed in the casket without the clothes being removed. Only a sheet is wrapped around it, over the clothes. The blood is part of the body and may not be separated from it in death.*

> *Where blood flows continually after death, the source of the flow is covered and not washed. The clothes which contain the blood that flowed after death are placed in the casket at the feet.[3]*

Lamm's information was convincing. However, scholarship required that Bonnie and I pursue this back to the time of Jesus.

It was during our search for the source of the ritual of not washing the blood of a man who dies a violent death that my perspective of Christianity and Judaism began to change. It was then that I realized that we could not pursue this subject back to the time of Jesus by pursuing Christianity's historical documents. To do this right, we had to follow the path of the Jewish faith into history.

Bonnie found that Lamm's work basically paraphrases the laws found in the Code of Jewish Law from the 16th century. The following quotes are from the more recent abridged version of the code:

> 9. *If a person falls and dies instantly, if his body was bruised and blood flowed from the wound, and there is apprehension that his life-blood was absorbed in his clothes, he should not be ritually cleansed, but interred in his garments and shoes. He should be wrapped in a sheet, above his garments. That sheet is called sobeb. It is customary to scoop up the earth at the spot where he fell, and if blood happens to be there or near by, all that earth is buried with him. Only the garments which he wore when he fell are buried with him, but if the blood splashed on other garments, or if he was placed upon pillows and sheets while the blood was flowing, all these need not be buried with him, but they must be thoroughly washed until no trace of blood remains, and the water is poured into the grave. If, however, the deceased did not bleed at all, his clothes should be removed, his body cleansed and wrapped in shrouds, as is done in the case of a natural death. . . .*

> *10. If blood has flown from the injured body, but it*
> *stopped and his clothes were removed, after which*
> *he recovered and lived for a few days and then*
> *died, he must be cleansed and dressed in shrouds.*
> *Even if his body is stained with the blood which*
> *issued forth from him, he must be cleansed, for*
> *the blood lost while being alive is not to be*
> *regarded as life-blood; we are only concerned*
> *with the blood which one loses while dying, for*
> *it is likely that this was his life-blood, or it is*
> *possible that life-blood was mixed with it.*[4]

There is no doubt that there was an exception to the normal custom of simply washing the dead prior to burial. If death is by violence and blood flows at the time of death, the victim does not undergo the ritual of washing, but the body is simply placed in a sheet and buried. This was true from the present to as far back as the 16th century, but in order to be certain that this ritual took place at the time of Jesus, we had to look further.

Pushing back to the time of Jesus in the New Testament brought forth no definite clues. It was only when I began to read the Pentateuch, the first five books of the Bible, that I began to get some insights regarding God's word to his people concerning blood. It was in Genesis that the first real evidence appeared:

> *Every moving thing that lives shall be food for you;*
> *and just as I gave you the green plants, I give you*
> *everything. Only, you shall not eat flesh with its life,*
> *that is, its blood.*
>
> *Genesis 9:3–4*

Again, I came across this theme, but expanded, in Leviticus (the third book of the Pentateuch):

*If anyone of the house of Israel or of the aliens who
reside among them eats any blood, I will set my face
against that person who eats blood, and will cut
that person off from the people. For the life of the
flesh is in the blood; and I have given it to you for
making atonement for your lives on the altar; for, as
life, it is the blood that makes atonement. Therefore
I have said to the people of Israel: No person among
you shall eat blood, nor shall any alien who resides
among you eat blood.*

Leviticus 17:10–12

The books of Genesis and Leviticus helped me to begin to
understand why the Jews had a concern for blood. However, not
eating blood was a concept totally different from not washing
blood from the body of a man who died a violent death. The
source of this ritual continued to elude me.

Eighteen months later I was still no closer to the source of
the Code of Jewish Law regarding not washing. Finally, through
the help of a close friend, I got the names of three academic
rabbis. The first two leads were not helpful. I was in my office
when I made the third call. I can remember my anticipation as I
asked, "Do you know the source of the Jewish custom of not
washing the blood from a victim who died from a violent death?"

The rabbi's response was an emphatic "Yes," and he continued
talking. "Do you have Danby's English translation of the Mishnah?"
I responded, "Yes." He continued, "Well look at Nazir, 7[2] page
289. Also look at Oholoth, 3[5] page 653. Read what it says about
blood and mingled blood." He went on to explain that the
concern was over the blood that flows at the time of death. With
regard to mingled blood, not only was the timing important but
the amount of blood was also important. It had to amount to a
quarter-log of blood that he defined as the contents of a small
wine cup. He went on to say that this blood would be considered

unclean. At the time I didn't really understand some of his terminology such as *unclean, quarter-log,* and *mingled blood.* It did not matter, for I now knew that I finally had a documented source of the nonwashing ritual. As I hung up the telephone, I was amazed at his immediate knowledge. I believe that this man knew the entire Mishnah by memory. The words of this scholarly rabbi still resound in my mind. I shall be forever grateful to him.

On arriving home that night, I went to the Mishnah. I found in the introduction a paragraph stating the Mishnah's origin. It read, "The Mishnah may be defined as a deposit of four centuries of Jewish religious and cultural activity in Palestine, beginning at some uncertain date (possibly during the earlier half of the second century B.C.) and ending with the close of the second century A.D."[5] It covered the period of time I was looking for—the life span of Jesus of Nazareth.

I went directly to the first passage that the rabbi had given me in Nazir. It was a list of body parts that rendered one "unclean," unclean as one would be if one touched a corpse.[6] Confused by what I read, I decided to move on to the second quote that the rabbi had given me. As I read the words from the Mishnah, I sensed the age of their composition. The author was qualifying and quantifying and thus defining the blood of a crucified man. I suddenly sensed that these lines of text had been waiting there for centuries, waiting to be rediscovered and understood by our own generation.

> *What counts as 'mingled blood?' If beneath a man that was crucified, whose blood gushes out, there was found a quarter-log of blood, it is unclean; but if beneath a corpse, whose blood drips out, there was found a quarter-log of blood, this is clean. R. Judah says: It is not so, but the blood that gushes out is clean and that which drips out is unclean.*

Note 1. According to one view, in the intermittent dripping of the blood the uncleanness of each drop in turn is nullified by its smallness in quantity; therefore the whole quarter-log is clean. According to the other view the slowness of its dripping is proof that it issued after death, and it is therefore unclean.[7]

It took me a long time to come to grasp the full meaning of these words, but it was all there—the explanation of why the blood of a man who dies a violent death is buried with the body. Mingled blood is the mixture of blood that issues while a man is alive with blood that issues from the man from the moment of death. The blood that issues while a man is alive is not important, but once it mingles with blood that flows from the moment of death it becomes mingled blood. For mingled blood to be considered unclean, it had to reach a certain volume as defined in the Mishnah. For mingled blood to be considered unclean, the quantity of blood had to at least amount to "a quarter-log" of blood. A log of blood is the contents of six eggs.[8] Therefore, a quarter-log is the contents of one and a half eggs. This amount is just enough to fill a small wine cup, exactly as the rabbi had described.

However, in order to comprehend why blood is buried with the body of a man who dies a violent death, I had to understand the biblical meaning of the term *unclean.* The following quote from Numbers, the fourth book of the Pentateuch, helped me to come to that understanding:

All who touch a corpse, the body of a human being who has died, and do not purify themselves, defile the tabernacle of the LORD; such persons shall be cut off from Israel. Since water for cleansing was not dashed on them, they remain unclean; their uncleanness is still on them.

Numbers 19:13

In other words, all who touch a corpse are rendered unclean (Numbers 19:13). If they do not undergo the ritual of cleansing (Numbers 19:2–9, 17–19), they defile the Holy Place and are cut off from Israel. With this understanding of the biblical meaning of the word *unclean,* I began to realize why the rabbi had referenced the list of body parts in Nazir.

The rabbi's first reference had to do with the first order of uncleanness with regard to a corpse. That meant that all the parts of the body that were listed in that passage of the Mishnah rendered one unclean by all means of contact, as unclean as one would be if one had touched a corpse. In other words, touching a body part was like touching a whole corpse, and it caused one to be unclean. Included in that list of body parts that convey uncleanness was "a half-log of blood."[9] That means that if you touch the blood from a corpse, you are as unclean as you would be if you had touched the corpse itself. Therefore, the blood as well as all the body parts must be buried with the body.

Considering a crucified man, the rabbi's second reference, Oholoth, was very specific. A quarter-log of mingled blood that flows from the body of a crucified person conveys uncleanness, the same uncleanness that the corpse conveys. Therefore, the mingled blood on the corpse of a crucified man must be buried with the body. The body is therefore not washed. *The Code of Jewish Law* makes it clear:

> *He should not be ritually cleansed, but interred in his garments and shoes. He should be wrapped in a sheet, above his garments. That sheet is called sobeb. It is customary to scoop up the earth at the spot where he fell, and if blood happens to be there or near by, all that earth is buried with him.*[10]

What is important about mingled blood is not the blood that comes forth during life but that which comes from a man at the time of death. ". . . for the blood lost while being alive is not to be regarded as life-blood; we are only concerned with the blood which one loses while dying, for it is likely that this was his life-blood, or it is possible that life-blood was mixed with it."[11] What is being described here is the "life-blood" of Genesis and Leviticus.

What is life-blood? I found a note in the Mishnah that defines it: "it is inferred that the blood which issues at the moment of death (which is what the Mishnah means by 'life-blood') is the blood that makes atonement."[12] In defining life-blood, the Mishnah refers to Leviticus 17:11. I reread the words from Leviticus:

> *For the life of the flesh is in the blood; and I have given it to you for making atonement for your lives on the altar; for, as life, it is the blood that makes atonement. Therefore I have said to the people of Israel: No person among you shall eat blood, nor shall any alien who resides among you eat blood.*
> *Leviticus 17:11–12*

I thought about these words as well as the Mishnah's definition of life-blood. I was beginning to understand the words of Genesis and Leviticus. They were the words of God. They were the words of the blood covenant that God established with the human race after the great flood. These words were taken seriously by God's people, the people of Israel, so seriously that the blood of all animals is drained before the flesh is eaten. This tradition lives on to this day among the Jewish people who partake of only kosher meats.

After learning about mingled blood, life-blood, and God's blood covenant with the people of Israel, the Jews, I read the Gospel of John with a different perspective:

*Then Pilate took Jesus and had him flogged. And the
soldiers wove a crown of thorns and put it on his head.*

John 19:1–2

There they crucified him.

John 19:18

*But when they came to Jesus and saw that he was
already dead, they did not break his legs. Instead,
one of the soldiers pierced his side with a spear, and
at once blood and water came out.*

John 19:33–34

I now realize that John's description of Jesus' death had a
different meaning to first-century Jews. I now understand what
they understood by his description. The man who hung on that
cross had upon him blood that flowed during life, mingled with
blood that flowed at the time of death. Mingled blood. It was
life-blood, the blood that makes atonement. It was unclean and
therefore had to be buried with him.

*They took the body of Jesus and wrapped it with the
spices in linen cloths, according to the burial custom
of the Jews.*

John 19:40

Jesus was buried according to the Jewish custom. The corpse
with its mingled blood was wrapped in "linen cloths" and buried.
Therefore, the shroud with its blood marks is consistent with the
history of how the Jews buried their dead at the time of Jesus.[13]
The search that John Reagan started us on was over.

Thomas would already know about Jewish burial customs
and he would agree that this search accurately presents the
customs of his time.

A Crucified Man

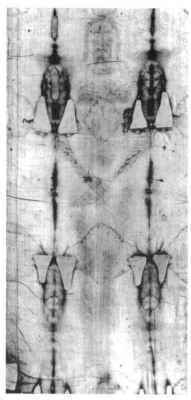

Figure 1

Image of the shroud
with blood mark
off the left elbow*

* The right elbow of the man covered by this cloth.

Figure 2

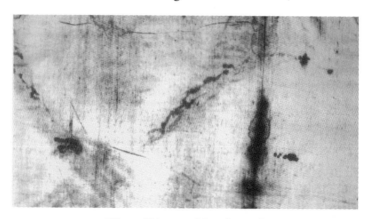

The off-image blood mark

Chapter Five

ב

Now that I knew that the shroud blood marks were a historical possibility, I wanted to see if Barbet's theory of blood transfers to cloth was reproducible. However, before beginning this work, I decided to pursue the study of a blood mark that had always intrigued me: the off-the-body-image blood mark located at the left elbow (Figure 1). I did not have an explanation as to how this blood mark got to its off-image position. Barbet had never mentioned it, and I never came across any information about it. In looking for answers, I went to the best authority I knew—Reverend Peter Rinaldi. He also was unaware of any existing explanation regarding the origin of this off-image blood mark.

The urge to understand the off-image blood mark caused me to hypothesize several theories regarding its origin, but none could be proven. Finally, one Saturday morning, I retrieved Father Donovan's full-size shroud images from my front closet. As I stood there, looking down at the off-image blood mark (Figure 2), I wondered what would happen if I placed the cloth over my own body. Would it give me more information? The next moment I was down on the rug with the frontal image over me. Once I was satisfied with the alignment of image to body, I looked over to see where the off-image blood mark was draping against my body. The location of the drape surprised me. The off-image blood mark was touching the back of my upper arm. I could hardly believe the logical interpretation of what I was seeing. This simple blood mark was leading me in a direction that I had never anticipated.

That same week, the whole family began working on a full-size tracing of the left arm and off-image blood mark (Figure 3). In going through the process of making the tracing, I followed the blood line from the forearm to where it ends its course at the off-image round spot. Never once is the continuity of this line broken. Once the tracing was completed, we then turned it over and laid it over one of us in the same way that we felt the shroud cloth had been laid upon a body (Figure 4). From this direct frontal view of the man, I noted that the off-image blood mark was not visible. Furthermore, what I saw through my camera was similar to what I saw on the shroud: an image with no sides. The shroud image is, therefore, similar to a direct frontal photograph of a man.

Figure 3

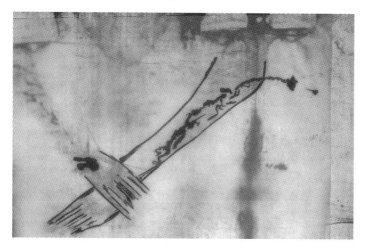

Full-size tracing of the off-image blood mark

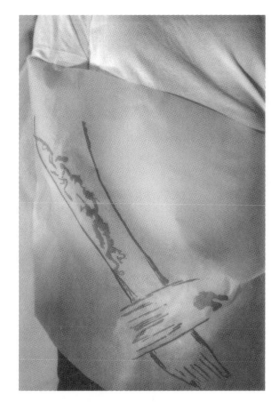

Figure 4

**Tracing laid
over a man**

On the side view of the same subject (Figure 5), the paper tracing drapes over the side of the body, simulating a cloth drape. From this information, it becomes obvious that the off-image blood mark was caused by the cloth touching the clot on the back of the upper arm as the cloth draped over the side of the body. At this point in the study, I realized that the other blood marks on the image translate into two-dimensional information, corresponding to the man's height and width. However, the off-image blood mark is graphic evidence pointing to yet a third dimension—depth: a three-dimensional figure had been under this cloth.

Finally, we placed the tracing and the arm of the volunteer in the crucifixion position (Figure 6). It was then that the last

Figure 5

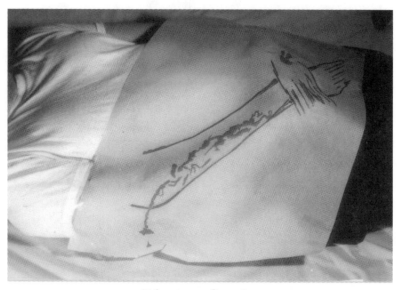

Side view of tracing

piece of the puzzle became obvious. The clotted blood on the back of the upper arm represents a prior blood flow that followed the force of gravity. The origin of the blood flow likely started at a wrist wound, which is not visible, and flowed down the forearm, past the elbow, and around the back of the upper arm collecting into a round pool of blood on the underside of the arm. From this pool, I could imagine that excess blood dripped off the body onto the ground. It reminded me of the description found in the Mishnah of the blood coming from a crucified man: ". . . but if beneath a corpse [of a crucified man], whose blood drips out, . . ."[1] Indeed, this blood mark is consistent with what was seen at a crucifixion. Furthermore, the path that this blood flow took is real, as real as it is to me every morning after I wet my hand and razor and begin to shave, as real as it would be to any of us who have experienced holding up wet hands

Figure 6

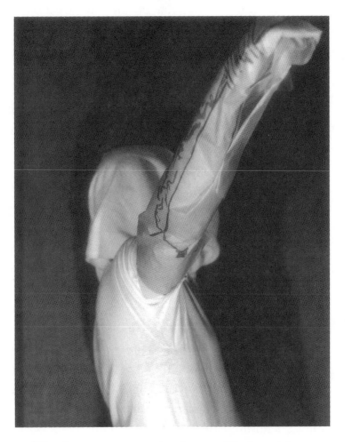

Tracing over a man in the crucified position

while waiting for someone to hand us a towel. In conclusion, the off-image blood mark indicates that the man of the shroud had been in the position of crucifixion. Barbet had made this same observation many years before when he studied another blood mark, that of the wrist. These blood marks of the shroud, therefore, demonstrate a consistent pattern.

The key to this whole study is the force of gravity. The blood had simply followed the pull of gravity, creating an unbroken line that ended in a small, suspended pool of blood. The man was later taken from the vertical position of crucifixion and placed on one end of the long shroud cloth, the other end then having been draped over the body. Again, gravity caused the side of the cloth to simply drape over the side of the victim, allowing the cloth to come into contact with the blood mark on the back of the upper arm. At that point, the shroud cloth touched the moist clot and acted much like a blotter in contact with wet ink: the moist clot left its imprint on the cloth. This blood mark was, therefore, the result of a simple contact process.

Once I understood the process of how the off-image blood mark was formed, I realized that this information brought me to an appreciation of the difference between the production of the blood marks and the creation of the image: (1) The off-image blood mark confirmed that the cloth touched the back of the upper arm. (2) The blood marks of the forearm also confirmed that the cloth had come in contact with the forearm. Therefore, the cloth had skin contact with the back of the upper arm as well as with the forearm. However, there is a major difference between the two. Where the cloth touched the forearm, the image of the forearm can be seen, but where the cloth touched the back of the upper arm, there is no image. Therefore, image formation had nothing to do with the cloth touching skin or sweat products. Why do I say this? Because there is no image on the cloth where the back of the upper arm came in contact with the cloth (Figures 1 and 2). Then what caused the image? I did not know. All I knew was that in contrast to the blood marks, the body image was not created by a contact process. If it had been, an image of the upper arm would be seen extending out as far as the off-image blood mark.

In summary, this off-image blood mark told me three things about the shroud: (1) The shroud cloth had covered the three-dimensional figure of a crucified man. (2) The blood marks were made by a contact process. (3) The image was not made by a contact process.[2]

Even now, when I think about the off-image blood mark, I still sense a certain excitement, for I know that there was a crucified man under this cloth. But would Thomas agree?

BLOOD TRANSFERS TO CLOTH

Chapter Six

Understanding the graphics of the off-image blood mark convinced me that the image marks of the shroud were definitely not made by a contact process. Then how did the image get on the cloth? I knew of no scientific explanation. Therefore, I decided to concentrate on the blood marks, something that I felt quite capable of pursuing.

I wanted to confirm what Barbet had inferred, that the blood marks on the shroud were the mirror images of blood clots on skin. In order to make this confirmation, it is important to first understand what Barbet means by "blood clots on skin." Clot formation is the biological reaction that blood undergoes when it leaves the body. (Clot formation also occurs inside the body, but this is not pertinent to our discussion.) Everyone experiences bleeding and clot formation sometime during life: Some form of trauma cuts open the skin, the wound appears, and then the blood begins to flow. Clot formation occurs when the liquid blood changes to a jellylike, solid, red form that no longer flows but sticks to the skin. After the clot is formed, it exudes a small amount of clear yellow serum for a short period of time. Finally, the red, jellylike mass dries and takes on a crusty appearance.

In an attempt to prove that blood clots transfer to cloth, I conceived a simple experiment.[1] First, I placed a thin transparent plastic sheet on a table. I then took fresh blood from a volunteer and immediately transferred it to the plastic surface in the form of eight small pools of blood, using about nine drops of blood to form each pool. I made oblong pools of blood and used the blood mark on the forehead of the shroud image for comparison.

.I numbered the pools of blood one through eight. I waited. It took about ten minutes for the liquid blood to clot.[2] After the clots were formed, it took a little over thirty minutes for the eight clots to start clot retraction.[3] (Clot retraction is a biological process whereby the clot actually shrinks in size, and while it does, it exudes or squeezes out a clear yellow fluid called serum.[4]) As the clots were getting slightly smaller, a clear yellow serum was accumulating around the clots. The clot retraction process was occurring to all eight clots at the same time. At this stage, each clot was a red, jellylike, oblong pool surrounded by a clear, pale-yellow halo.

I had also prepared eight small squares of linen cloth to place over these eight blood clots. Exactly thirty minutes from the time that the blood was withdrawn from the volunteer, I covered the first clot with cloth. I covered the second clot thirty minutes later and so on until I had covered each clot in sequential order at half-hour intervals. Four hours from the time that I had drawn the blood, I covered the last clot with a linen square. Twenty-four hours later, I lifted the squares of linen from the plastic surface. A hard, crusted, dry clot covered each cloth. I took a penny and scraped off the excess crusted blood. When I compared the bloodstained cloths to the forehead clot of the shroud, I was both amazed and disappointed at what I saw (Figure 1).

As I looked at the outcome of this simple experiment, I could see that the results of the transfers from clots to cloth were not as neat as the blood mark of the forehead. The forehead clot on the

Figure 1

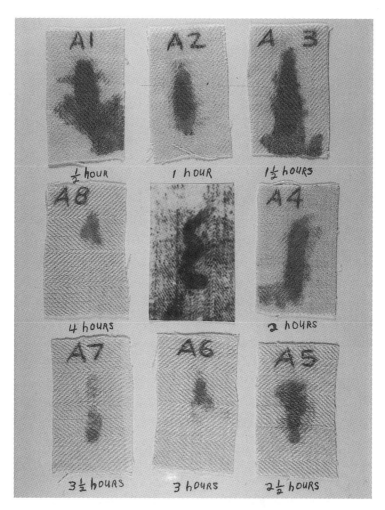

Blood clots with serum lines
Experiment conducted on a horizontal surface

shroud shows what looked like a serum line about the edge, but overall it was more precise than the clot transfers of the experiment. I just sat there at the table looking at the results, wondering why the discrepancy, when suddenly, in the middle of another thought, I realized that I had made a mistake in the design of the experiment. The fact was that the blood clotted on a horizontal surface. The horizontal position allowed the exuded serum to accumulate around the clots and cause an uneven transfer to cloth. But the man of the shroud did not die in the horizontal position; rather, he died in the vertical position of crucifixion, and the blood clotted on his skin while he was still in this position.

I could hardly wait to start the experiment over again. This time, within the first half hour after blood withdrawal, I placed the eight clots in a vertical position. This was time enough to allow for clot formation. As a result, the clots kept their shape and clung to the vertical surface of the plastic surface. After a short time, clot retraction began to occur, and the clear yellow serum was being exuded from the clots. I watched in amazement as the serum dripped down the vertical wall of clear plastic, leaving behind neat, moist, red, jellylike clots. At the same time that I placed the clots in the vertical position, I placed a linen cloth on the first clot. I continued doing this at half-hour intervals until all eight clots were covered, just as I had done with the first experiment. However, the clots no longer collected the pools of excess serum about them as they had in the previous study. After twenty-four hours, I turned the cloths over and found dry, crusted clots (Figure 2). I removed the crust as before. These clot transfers were neat and were more similar to the forehead blood mark (Figure 3). I did a shorter experiment on normal skin, and the results were similar (Figure 4). Therefore, I confirmed Barbet's deduction that some of the shroud blood marks were clots that were transferred to cloth.

As I watched the clot-to-cloth transfers take place, it became obvious that it was the moisture of the remaining serum at the surface of the clots that allowed the transfers to take place. As soon as a cloth was placed over a clot, I would first see the clear

Figure 2

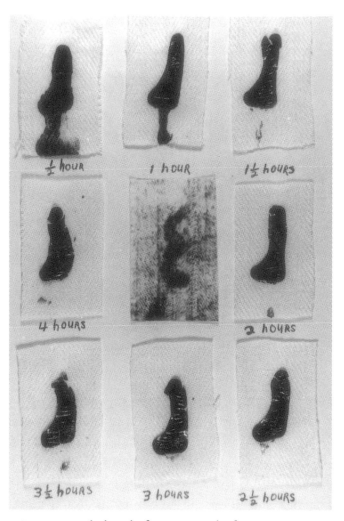

Dry crusted clots before removal of excess crust

yellow serum pass through the cloth giving it a wet appearance. This was followed by the red blood cells of the clot that gave it its final red appearance as the soak-through came to its completion. In the case of the man of the shroud, some of the excess

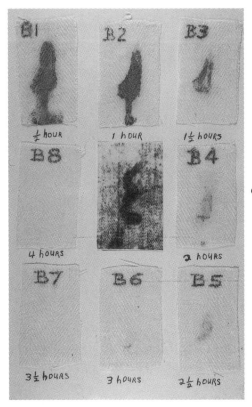

Figure 3

Blood clots
with
neat clot transfers
to cloth,
experiment conducted
on a vertical surface

serum dripped away from the clots while the body was in the vertical position. What remained on the skin were neat appearing clots still moistened by the remaining serum, which enabled the clots to seep into the shroud cloth at the time of burial.

I could also see from the experiment that there was a time limit on the ability of the clots to transfer to cloth (Figures 3 and 4). At room temperature, transfers could take place up to one and a half hours after the blood was taken from the volunteer. Over time, as the moisture evaporated from the clot, the clot lost its ability to transfer to cloth. The clot became too dry, and as a result, it could no longer soak into the fibers of the linen. One and a half hours after the time of blood withdrawal, the clot no

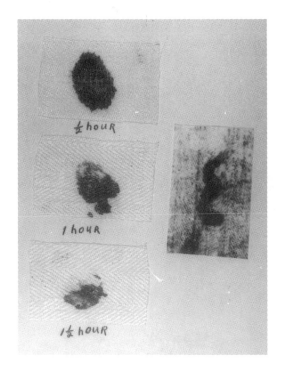

Figure 4

**Blood stains
transferred
from skin**

longer made a transfer to cloth (Figures 3 and 4). When the clots are moistened artificially with normal saline, this time can be extended up to two hours (Figure 5).[5] In the case of a crucified man, it may be possible that body sweat could have provided extra moisture.[6]

The experiment of clot transfer to cloth, performed on a plastic surface and normal skin, was not intended to duplicate the actual event, but was done so that this event could be better understood. In doing this experiment, I realized that the ability of the moist clot to transfer to cloth would be affected by many factors, such as temperature, humidity, movement of ambient air, skin moisture, and skin temperature. With regard to the man of the shroud, these are all unknown factors. Furthermore, the timing of the movement of the body from a vertical to the horizontal position could affect the accumulation of serum deposit

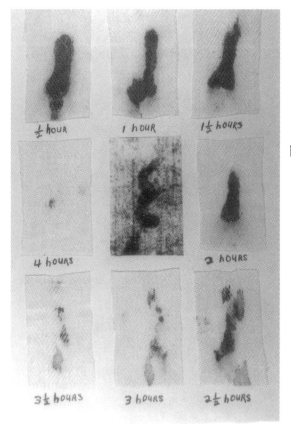

½ hour   1 hour   1½ hours

4 hours   2 hours

3¼ hours   3 hours   2½ hours

Figure 5

Blood clots
moistened
by normal saline

about the clots and ultimately affect the outcome of clot to cloth transfer. Regardless of all these unknowns, I learned that moist clots, relieved of some, but not all, of their serum by the vertical position of crucifixion, could easily have been transferred to cloth within one and a half hours and possibly up to two hours from the time of the death of the man of the shroud.

What is even more amazing about this timetable is that it corresponds to the gospel account of Jesus' death and burial. The time of death was ". . . three in the afternoon"(Luke 23:44). His burial took place thereafter: "He [Joseph] took it [the body] down, wrapped it in a shroud and put him in a tomb. . . . It was

Preparation Day and the sabbath was imminent" (Luke 23: 53–54, *The Jerusalem Bible*). The time of burial had to take place before the Sabbath because, according to the Mishnah, no part of the body may be moved on the Sabbath.[7] The beginning of the Sabbath was between 5 and 6 P.M. (March and April Sabbath times in Jerusalem).[8]

As I continued to study the subtleties of the shroud's blood marks, I began to realize that the serum from the clots on the man of the shroud did not all drip away as it did on the vertical plastic surface experiment, but rather clung to the skin. For example, in contrast to the neat, barely visible serum lines around the blood mark of the forehead are the more visible serum lines around the blood mark of the wrist (Figures 6 and 7). The location of the wrist wound and its association with the trauma incurred at the wrist explain some of the reasons for the difference.

These serum lines, similar to the serum lines of the first plastic surface experiment (Figure 8), tell another part of the story. Crucifixion, as noted in the Mishnah, was a dynamic, ongoing process of blood dripping or gushing from the crucified. Eventually, the blood on the surface of the body would clot, exude serum, and dry up. But as long as life was maintained, bleeding would continue from the open wounds. All of the serum did not drain away as it did in my simple plastic surface experiment, but some did accumulate on the skin adjacent to the clots. When death finally came, the last blood flows of the wrist clotted and then retracted, and the exuded serum clung to the adjacent skin. The blood mark of the wrist, as seen on the shroud cloth, is the mirror image of that last event. Details like this convinced Barbet, the surgeon, that the blood marks of the shroud represent mirror images of clotted blood. Paint does not separate and create the serum lines that are seen here (Figure 7). Only blood does this.

When I called Vern Miller in 1991 to ask him for some shroud photos, he reminded me of the work he had done in 1978 regarding the blood marks. Using ultraviolet fluorescence photography, he took pictures of the shroud and found that there

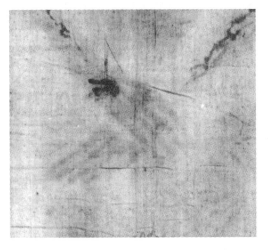

Figure 6

Blood mark at the wrist

Figure 7

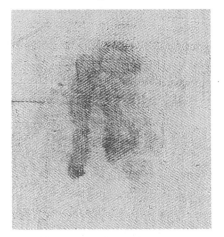

Blood mark at the wrist with surrounding serum lines

Figure 8

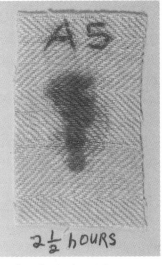

Blood mark with serum lines from Figure 1

were halos of fluorescence around some of the blood marks.[9] For example, there were "clear fluorescing borders around the hand wound blood stains."[10] He went on to say that he was never able to reproduce his findings using blood. In our discussion, I realized that he had not photographed any blood samples with serum lines. In response, I sent Miller the blood marks with serum lines (Figure 1), which were the result of my 1983 transfer experiments. He took pictures of these and found that the blood marks with the serum lines did indeed fluoresce, reproducing the fluorescent halos that he had found around some of the blood marks of the shroud. Because of his persistence in wanting to understand the reason for the fluorescent halos about the shroud blood marks, Vern Miller visually reconfirmed Alan Adler's blood chemistry [11] and my studies as well as the original observations of clot-to-cloth transfers made by Barbet. Indeed, the blood marks of the shroud demonstrate that they had exuded serum.

Having worked in a hospital emergency room, I have had many personal encounters with bleeding patients. People with head injuries tend to bleed profusely because the scalp is very vascular. These patients are usually covered with blood even when the head wound is very small. After examining the numerous blood flows on the head and the face of the man of the shroud, I believe that he must have been completely covered with blood. This blood eventually dried and, therefore, made no transfer to cloth. The only blood clots that transferred to the shroud were those that contained moisture. Those blood clots would have resulted from the last blood flows that occurred near and at the time of death. Therefore, the blood-clot transfers that we see on the shroud are what the Mishnah defines as mingled blood.[12]

Barbet mentions in his book that he believed that while the body was wrapped, it was bathed in a watery atmosphere causing the dry clots on the skin to be damp once more.[13] To verify his suggestion, I added normal saline to each clot. But this only prolonged the transfer of neat clots to cloth from one and a half to two hours. After two hours, when the clots had dried, moistening them did not produce satisfactory transfers (Figure 5). Retrospectively, I can understand why Barbet surmised that the clots were remoistened in the cave. He knew that moist clots are very easily disturbed. He also knew that if a man was taken from the vertical position of crucifixion and placed on a cloth, the clots on his body would be easily disturbed. Finally, he knew that there is no sign of disturbed clots on the shroud.

What Barbet did not realize was that the blood of the shroud is mingled blood. Because there are no signs that the blood marks of the shroud were disturbed, I believe that it is reasonable to make the following assumption: The work of moving the man from the crucified position to the shroud was done by people who took great care not to disturb the moist blood clots that covered the body of this man. Historically, the only people who would make such an effort are the people of Israel. Therefore, this effort suggests that this was a Jewish burial.

In summary, as I did this study, I learned four things about the blood marks of the shroud: (1) I was able to confirm Barbet's observation that blood clots transfer to cloth as mirror images of themselves. (2) The neatness of some of the transfers is likely related to the fact that the man of the shroud died in the vertical position. (3) The ability of clots to transfer to cloth at room temperature is about one and a half to two hours, depending on available moisture. These times coincide closely with the gospel timetable of the death and burial of Jesus. (4) The undisturbed clot transfers seen on the shroud cloth suggest that this was a Jewish burial.

This gives Thomas more to think about.

BEYOND OUR ORDINARY UNDERSTANDING OF SPACE AND TIME

Chapter Seven

Figure 1

Shroud face,
positive image

For many years the positive image of the shroud face (Figure 1) hung on my office wall. Almost every day I looked across my desk at that face, sometimes partially closing my eyes as I gazed at the image, wondering if the face held some secret. During those years, I would always delight in showing any interested observer the blood marks of the face and hair, the contusion under the right eye, and the way the face would seem to follow me as I walked from one side of the room to the other.

In 1986, I discovered something new. Over time, as I would observe the blood of the forehead and hair, I wondered if the blood came out a little too far on either side of the face. I wondered if it were not the same phenomenon as is seen at the off-image blood mark at the left elbow. Eventually I took the life-size picture of the shroud face from the wall and brought it home. I asked my daughters, Catherine and Marguerite, to outline on tracing paper the blood marks of the forehead and hair. I also asked them to trace the position of the eyes and nose. I then had Catherine make a cutout of the tracing, remove the paper within the outlined blood marks, and make holes at the eyes that would be large enough to see through. When she finished, I took her work and went to a mirror and placed the tracing paper with its cutout over my face, aligning the eyes and nose of the figure with my own. As I looked through the eye slits at the reflection of the paper that covered my face, I was stunned by what I saw. Wanting confirmation from an objective observer regarding the reflection in the mirror, I sent the cutout to Alan Adler with the following instructions: "Go to a mirror, then align and wrap the cutout on your face, and let me know what you think you are looking at."

He called back. "When I first saw your cutout, I thought that you had finally lost your mind and had started playing with paper dolls. But I decided that I'd humor you and play along. I went to the mirror to look, and I couldn't believe what I saw. The blood is not on the hair. It's on the sides of the face!" Alan came to the same conclusion as I had. It was as simple as cutting out paper dolls, but the information helps us to better understand the shroud.

Visually reproducing this was fairly simple. All I needed was a bearded man. Reverend Dan Twomey of my own parish volunteered. It was while I was taking the first picture of Father Dan as he was sitting at my dining-room table that I suddenly realized that I had made a mistake. I was not working with a vertical image on the shroud, but with a horizontal image, so I asked him if he would lie down (Figure 2) so that I could retake his picture in the correct position. Using my full-size photograph of the

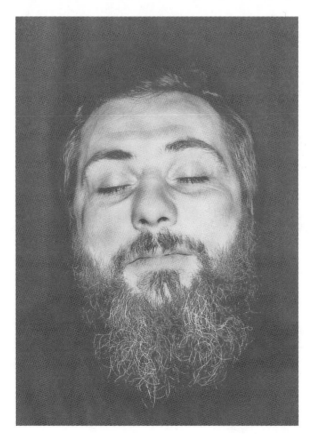

Figure 2

Man's face in a lying position

shroud face, we had already prepared another cutout of the blood marks of the face and hair, but this time we used cloth (Figure 3). I draped the cloth with the cutout of the blood marks over Father Dan's face (Figure 4), aligning his eyes and nose with that of the tracing. While the cloth was over his face, I applied paint to his skin through each blood-mark cutout. I then removed the

Figure 3   **Figure 4**

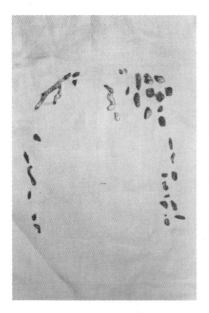
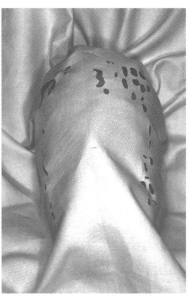

Cutout of the blood marks
of the face and hair
of the shroud

Cutout of the blood marks
draped over a man's face

cloth from his face. The painted blood marks graphically demonstrated that all the blood marks seen on the hair of the shroud image had been originally on the face. Yes, they had been on the temples and cheeks of the man who had been under the shroud (Figure 5). The blood marks are consistent with a cloth having been draped and sufficiently tucked over a man's face covered with moist clots. The transfer of blood to cloth was a simple contact process. This blood went onto the cloth before the image (see page 62).

These same blood marks of the face also told me something about the facial image: the shroud cloth had been in intimate contact not only with the front of the face but also with the sides of the face (Figure 5). Yet despite the intimate contact that the shroud cloth had with the temples and cheeks, no images of the sides of the face are seen (Figure 1). In contrast, if images had been produced where the shroud cloth came in contact with the sides of the face, the resulting facial image would have been markedly distorted. The cheeks and temples would have extended out to the blood marks seen in the hair. It would have looked like Vignon's experiment, that of the flattened face that Bonnie and I saw in Turin in 1978.

Only now do I finally realize that Vignon's experiment with aloes and ammonia[1] was simply a straightforward contact process. That is why the nose and cheeks of the experiment were broad and distorted. The cloth had touched the sides of the nose and draped over the roundness of the cheeks and temples. That resulted in the accentuated broad flat face. But the nose and cheeks of the shroud are not broadened, and the face of the shroud image is not grotesque. Rather, what you see is the frontal view of a normal face, the same frontal view that you would see of yourself in a mirror or photograph. What does the absence of the images of the sides of the shroud face mean? It means that the shroud image could not possibly have been formed by a cloth-to-body contact process. Then what had caused the image? I did not know, but as time passed, I began to realize that the blood on the face and hair had more to reveal about the image.

As I contemplated the facial image and the graphics of the blood marks, the chasm between the two grew deeper and wider until I could no longer look upon the shroud image in the same

Figure 5

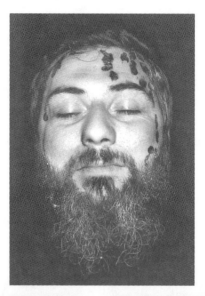

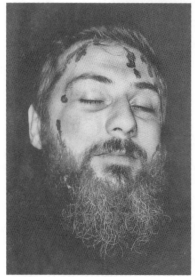 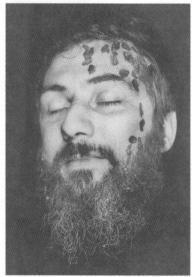

Blood marks painted on the man's face
through the cutout

way. The key to the puzzle—a puzzle that I previously had not even known existed—was the spatial relationship of the cloth to the face that it covered. I now understood that to produce the blood marks that are seen on the face and hair of the shroud, the shroud cloth had to be draped over a three-dimensional face that was covered by moist blood clots. Because of this understanding, I began to look at the shroud's facial image from a different point of view. I started to recognize the obvious: the temples and the cheeks of the image do not exhibit the blood marks that had been on the face of the man who had been covered by the shroud. Those blood marks are now out in the hair. Furthermore, if the blood marks were on the face of the shroud image, the final facial image would be more like Figure 5 instead of Figure 1.

The relationship of the blood marks to the facial image (Figure 6) demanded an answer to the following question: What does this lack of congruence say with regard to image formation? It says that image formation did not take place at the time that the cloth was draped over the face. Why? Because the draped cloth that was touching the temples and the cheeks carries the mirror image of the moist blood clots that were originally on the draped man's temples and cheeks. These blood marks are now in the hair that falls along the sides of the face (Figure 1).

Furthermore, and most important, the direct frontal view of the cheeks and temples of the facial image lies in between the blood marks that were originally on the temples of the man draped by the shroud (Figure 6). It seems that the facial image was created not at the time of the draping, but at a time when the cloth was stretched out and a negative photograph of the face appeared on the flattened cloth between the blood marks. The visual information at hand tells its own story. The production of the blood marks and the formation of the body image are much more than two different phenomena each caused by a different

Figure 6

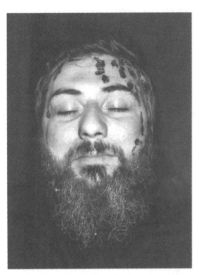

Positive

Negative

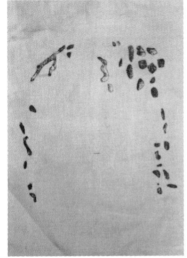

Cutout

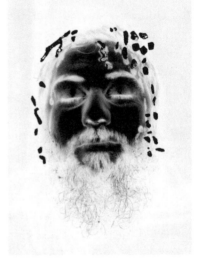

Cutout superimposed
over negative

process. They really tell us something more: When the transfer of blood to cloth took place, the cloth was draped and sufficiently tucked to cause the transfer; the cloth was in one position. When the image was formed, it seems that the cloth was in a second position—stretched out flat. Therefore, the cloth had to have been spatially in two separate positions. Events separate in space and separate in time![2]

For a while I believed that this was the final conclusion to the study—in order to produce the blood marks and create the image the cloth had to have been spatially in two separate positions, events separate in space and separate in time. But now I realize that I was wrong about this conclusion for there is much more to be understood. Thomas wanted to go beyond seeing and wanted to touch in order to confirm the experience. In the same spirit, I ask you to join me in a simple experiment so that you may fully experience what is happening here. The experiment will help you understand that a real and very special event took place on the shroud. This event is a reflection of what Thomas experienced. You will eventually understand but it is important that you now continue to carefully follow along step by step.

First we need to review some of the photographs. Look at Figure 1 in this chapter. See where the hair falls along the sides of the face, and there in the hair you also see the blood marks that were originally on the temples and cheeks of the man that was under the shroud as is seen in Figure 5. Look at these figures for a moment and then go back to Figure 1. Note that there is little blood on the temples and on the cheeks of Figure 1 and that the blood that was originally there (Figure 5) is now out on the hair. Continue to study these photographs until you fully understand them and then you can start the experiment. Furthermore please bear with me for the moment and for the sake of the experiment make up any method you might imagine—radiation, heat, etc.—that may have been the source of energy that caused the body-to-cloth transfer resulting in the image. With that in mind, let us start.

Experiment: To best understand the production of the blood marks and creation of the image, I will suggest that you take a cloth napkin and place it over your face while lying on your back. Place it so that the cloth touches the temples and cheeks of your face. Now place your fingers on the napkin over the areas where your forehead meets your temples. It was there at the curves of your face (forehead-temple areas) (Figure 5) where the shroud touched the moist blood clots and they were soaked up into the cloth. Now while you are lying there ask yourself how could the image of the hair, which is on the sides of the head (see Figure 1), get onto the cloth while the cloth was still clinging to your forehead-temple areas. Whatever sources of energy you chose, I believe that you will find the image transfer of hair to cloth difficult while the cloth is still lying on your temples and cheeks.

The only way to rationalize what happened is to see blood transfer and image formation as two separate events as was discussed earlier in this chapter. First, with the cloth draped and sufficiently tucked, there is a transfer of blood to cloth. The second event would take place once you stretch and straighten the cloth out as if it were a flat mirror in front of your face. Then the image would be transferred onto the flat surfaces of the cloth as if you were looking into a mirror and seeing your face with the long hair hanging down along the sides.* But please remember, when you stretch out the cloth you bring the blood that was on the forehead-temple areas (see Figure 6) out to the sides of your face. Now you can use your chosen method (energy source) to transfer the features of your face and hair to the cloth. This step-by-step process simply gives us a way of understanding why we

---

* The mirror example is just a way of explaining a difficult concept and is not to be interpreted in any other way.

see the blood in the hair when it actually originated from the temples and cheeks of the man under the cloth.

The draping of the cloth over the face onto moist blood clots on the temples and cheeks caused the blood marks that you see. (Figure 1) It is straightforward contact process—cloth coming into contact with moist blood clots that soak into it leaving a specific pattern. This experiment can be reproduced at any time using the techniques presented in the first part of this chapter. After such an experiment I believe it is safe to say that even Thomas would conclude that the blood marks on this cloth were a natural phenomenon.

But image formation is different and requires an additional step. For the image of the face and hair to be transferred to the cloth we have to assume that the cloth was flattened out over the body as the image was being transferred from body to cloth. As a result, it seems as if the cloth was flattened out and a negative photo was taken of the face. The bloodmarks, originally on the temples and cheeks of the man under the cloth, now appear to be in the hair of the image. Hopefully this experiment helps you to understand the dilemma of body-to-cloth image transfer and provides a logical way to visualize it, at least for the moment.

But we have no proof that the cloth moved. The blood-to-body alignment is perfect and indicates no movement. The blood marks tell us that this cloth was draped and sufficiently tucked to cause the blood marks that are seen. Can we assume that someone then flattened it? We cannot. Therefore we are left with a cloth that was draped over a body and somehow the image got onto the cloth in a manner that defies our normal under-standing of image transfer, and defies our normal understanding of space and time. Why? Because we cannot reconcile having the same segment of cloth on two areas of the head simultaneously (at the same time): First on the forehead-temple areas where it soaked up the blood clots and second, at the sides of the face where hair is falling. We cannot reconcile that the falling hair transferred its image to that very same space of cloth that should still be on the forehead-temple areas.

In other words the image got on the cloth without the movement of cloth into a position that would allow for transfer in a way that we can understand. *This transfer of body to cloth that resulted in an image did not follow our ordinary understanding of space and time.*

Now it is important that we get back to the form of energy that you chose to cause the body-to-cloth transfer that results in a negative image. What form of energy would do this? First of all, one has to decide whether the energy comes from the body or from an outside source. What kind of energy came from a cold corpse that could cause such an image? None has ever been demonstrated. If an outside source of energy caused the image, where did it come from and what was it? None has ever been produced that leaves us with such a complex image as we see on the shroud. The bottom line is not what people say or speculate, but whatever form of energy that is theorized has to produce the complex image of the shroud (have all the same qualities— photo, 3D quality, X-ray) and produce this image so that it is also the same as the shroud image at the microscopic fiber level. To be consistent we have to follow the Thomas rule of first demanding to see results before believing what anyone says. Furthermore, we would need evidence that this form of energy was available centuries ago.

Terms such as radiation, heat, X-radiation, autoradiography, dematerialization, corona discharge, photography, vaporizations, vertically collimated radiation, microbes, contact—and the list goes on—have all been used by scientists in an attempt to understand the energy source that caused this image. There is some truth that lies in some of these theories, but none have been able to produce the shroud image with all its qualities and fulfill the criteria of being the same as the shroud at the microscopic level.

This shroud image is an enigma, and the more one looks, the more complex the image becomes. Most important, in over one hundred years since 1898 when Secondo Pia took the first photograph that started the search for a natural cause, no one has been able to accomplish the feat of reproducing it. We do not understand the mechanics of body-to-cloth position that accounts for a transfer of the image from body to cloth, nor do we know what the source of energy is that ultimately caused the image. Therefore, it is reasonable to say at this time that the shroud image remains a wonder without explanation. Would Thomas agree? I think so.

THE UPRIGHT MAN

Chapter Eight

I had thought about it since 1986 when I did my paper on the blood marks on the face. However, I had never put my thoughts down in writing until now. As I held up to the light a transparency of the shroud face (Figure 1), I was reminded that the image and the blood marks were telling their own story. It was all so logical, and it seemed as if it had all been planned for the human mind to contemplate.

When the insight first came, I was in my living room comparing the negative photograph of Father Dan's face to my transparency of the shroud face as it is seen on the cloth. As I held the negative of Dan's face (Figure 2) up to the light, I was struck by the fact that his image was not similar to the shroud image. On the shroud face, there was light around the eyes, under the nose, at the lips; Dan's face was a bland gray, with no striking differences of shades of gray as seen on the shroud image. They were not the same. What was wrong? Knowing that the shroud image has photographic qualities since Pia's first photograph in 1898, I made every effort to reproduce a negative that would simulate it. (The shroud image is now believed to be more than a negative not only because of VP8 image analysis, but

Figure 1   **Figure 2**

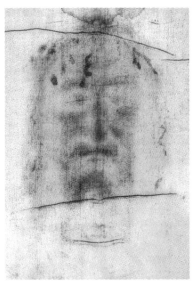
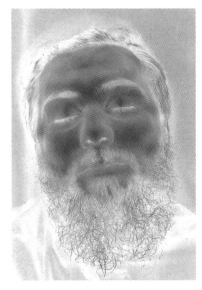

Shroud face,   **Negative image of face,**
negative image   **lying position**

because it seems to have some of the qualities that x-rays have. (See p. 54) However, the study of the photographic qualities of the shroud image has revealed the remarkable positive and negative images that continue to produce more information about the shroud.) I even placed the bearded volunteer in the supine position (lying on his back) so as to best imitate the image of the shroud. Disappointed in my findings, I began to look through all my negatives until I came across another negative of Dan's face. In awe, I sat there. There was no denying it. The light areas around the eyes, between the lips, and under the nose were all there. Dan's face (Figure 3) had very similar characteristics to the shroud face except for some of the shading of the hair. This negative of Dan had been photographed differently than Figure 2.

Figure 1 | Figure 3

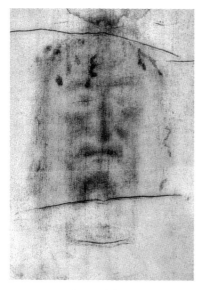

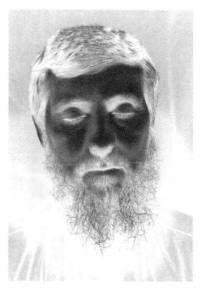

Shroud face,
negative image

Negative image of face,
upright position

In taking pictures of Father Dan, it was my original intention to photograph him lying on his back, the position that I felt best simulated the image of the man of the shroud. However, by mistake, I first took a picture of Dan's face in the upright position. It was this negative of Dan's face in the upright position that looked very much like the face of the shroud image. What appear like shadows of the shroud's facial image, indicate that the man of the shroud is upright rather than in the lying position, the position of burial.

I later studied the negatives of Dan's face. After trial and error, the conclusions were simple enough, and they were easily reproducible. If a source of light is from above, as it usually is in daily life, and a person is upright, there are shadows (light areas) around the eyes, under the nose, and about the lips (Figure 3).

Figure 4   Figure 5

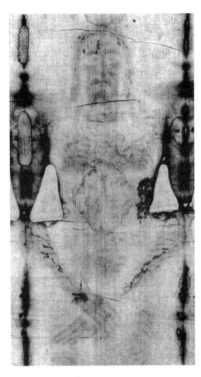
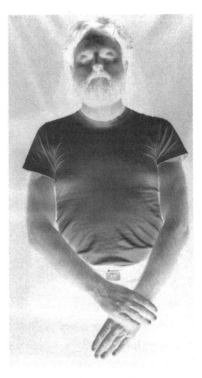

Frontal image   Negative image of a man,
of the shroud,   upright position,
negative image   light coming from above

(The shroud face carries other areas that appear like shadows that
correspond to facial swellings caused by a beating. See Barbet
Chapter 1.) If an individual is lying on his or her back and the
light source is from above, there are virtually no shadows (Figure
2). After further observation, I found other areas that appear like
shadows (light areas) on the shroud image (Figure 4). These are
light areas under the hair, at the neck, under the pectoral muscles
of the chest, and under the hands. All these light areas seen on
the shroud image can be seen on the negative image of a man

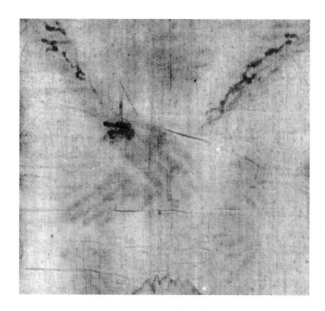

Figure 6

**Hands
of the
shroud
image,
negative
image**

(Figure 5). As long as the light is from above and the man is upright, the shadows (light areas) are similar to those of the shroud. Shadows (light areas) of the negative can be seen under the neck, under the pectorals, and at the hands (Figure 5). If we look at the hands of the shroud image (Figure 6), we can easily see what appear like shadows (light areas) between the fingers and on the underside of the hand with the visible wrist wound. This is nicely reproduced on an upright negative image of a man with the light source coming from above (Figure 7). In contrast, there are no shadows (light areas) seen on the negative image of the hands when the man is in the supine (lying) position and the light is from above (Figure 8). Therefore, all these areas that resemble shadows seen on the image of the shroud are also seen on a negative photograph of a man in the upright position with the source of light coming from above. It is specifically because the shroud image has photographic qualities that we are able to determine that this is an image of an upright man. Does this mean that the shroud image was formed by light and that the

Figure 7

**Negative image
of hands,
upright position**

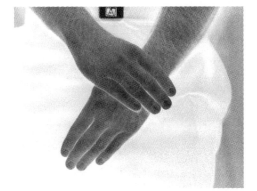

Figure 8

**Negative image
of hands,
lying position**

shroud image is a straightforward photograph? No, the shroud image is more complex than a photograph and the truth is that no one knows how this image was formed. (To be specific if one should put the photographs of this chapter, except for the shroud images, into a VP8 image analyzer, not one of them would give the three dimensional quality that the shroud does because photographs of people are not the same as the shroud image. see p. 54) This study is simply an observation made about the light areas of the shroud image (Figure 4) and these light areas look like shadows on the positive image (Figure 15). Because of what looks like shadows on the face and body of the positive image (Figure 15) it appears that this is an image of an upright man.

Figure 9

Negative front image
of long hair,
upright position

Figure 10

Negative back image
of long hair,
upright position

Figure 11A

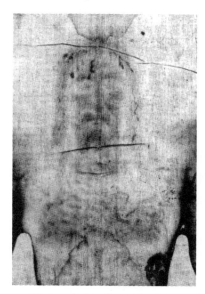

Hair of the front image,
negative image

Figure 11B

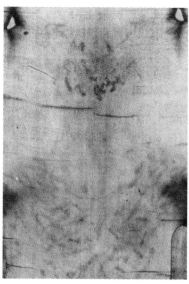

Hair of the back image,
negative image

Figure 9   **Figure 12**

   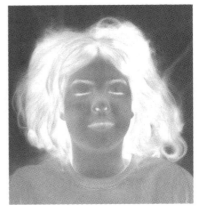

Negative front image   Negative front image
of long hair,   of long hair,
upright position   lying position

I then searched for consistencies other than what look like shadows that would correspond to an upright man. As I looked over the frontal image of the shroud, I suddenly became aware of the obvious. Again, another answer was found at the face of the image. This time it was the hair. The hair flows down on both sides of the face following the force of gravity. Looking at the back image I could see that the same was true. The hair flows over the shoulders and down the back.

In order to confirm these findings, I did a simple experiment. Figures 9, 10, 11A, 11B, and 12 tell the story. Figures 9 and 10 are the negative imprints of the front and back of an upright volunteer with long hair. The hair falls along the sides of the face to the shoulders and down the back. The hair of these images is consistent with that of the shroud (Figures 11A and 11B). Figure 12 is the negative image of the same person (taken at another time) in the supine, or lying, position. The hair falls to the ground rather than to the shoulders. (Again this is simply an

observation that is made using photographs as a means of illus-
tration to better understand the image, just as was done with the
photographs used to study the light areas on the shroud image.
In this case photographs of the volunteer will likely not give the
three dimensional quality of the hair falling which the shroud
image gives in a VP8 image analyzer.[1] Photographs of people are
not the same as the shroud image (See p. 54). It is simple
enough. Long hair responds to gravitational force and takes on a
typical appearance that is familiar to everyone. The hair of the
man of the shroud is that of an upright man.

The above observations indicate that this is not the image
of a man lying in burial but is the image of an upright man.
These observations require no chemical test, no technical
instruments and no scientific training. It is simply there for you
to see. Some will see it and some will not. I had been studying
the shroud for eight years before I noted these findings, and for
me it is now plain as day. Why didn't I see them before? I had
been blinded by my own conviction that this was the image of
a man who was laid in burial. The blood marks are consistent
with that conviction. Therefore I assumed that the image was
the same. I was wrong. I have come to learn that the more we
assume about the shroud image, the greater the risk of
distancing ourselves from its message.

Upright, yes, but not standing. The position of the soles of
the feet (Figure 13 & 14) indicate that the image of the man of
the shroud is not in the standing position. This whole experience
reminded me of a lecture on Barbet's studies of the shroud that I
had given many years before to a group of physicians. After the
lecture, one of the physicians approached me. He looked puzzled
and said emphatically, "It seems as if the man is suspended in
midair." At the time I said "Yes." But I really did not understand
what he had seen. He saw what it took me years to see: the image
of a man who is upright and suspended in midair.[2]

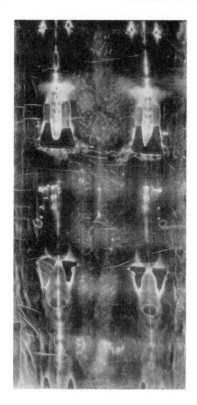

Figure 13

Back image
of the shroud,
positive image
backlighted

Figure 14

Soles of the feet
of the shroud,
positive image
backlighted

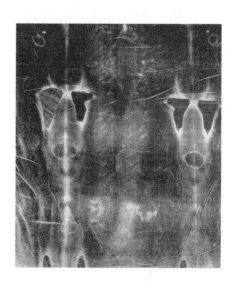

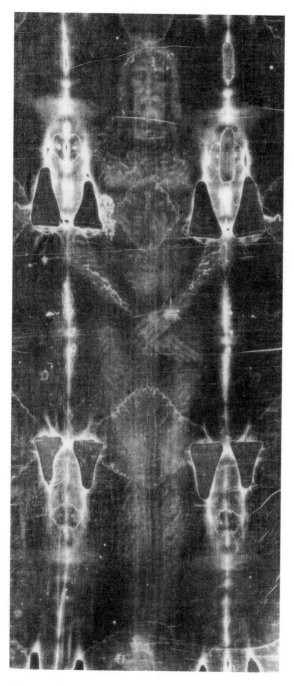

Figure 15: Front of shroud, positive image

What does the upright man mean from a scientific perspective? From the point of view of understanding body-to-cloth image transfer, the upright man complicates the process as much and probably more than the problem of body-to-cloth position as described in chapter 7. In attempting to understand the mechanics of body-to-cloth position and the source of energy that caused the image, questions always arise such as, how could the cloth maintain alignment with the blood marks of the man if he moved from a lying to an upright position? Where did the light come from? There are no answers to such questions because no one knows how the image was formed. For those of us who have attempted to discover a natural phenomenon as the cause of the image, the upright man adds another hurdle in the efforts to understand the mechanics (cloth-to-body relationship) of the event. Therefore, at this time, the creation of the image remains a wonder without explanation.

Finally what does the upright man mean from a religious perspective? Let's wait to see how Thomas would interpret this.

THE THOMAS REPORT

Chapter Nine

Now Thomas had the advantage of being at the right place at the right time when it comes to hard evidence for the resurrection. We do not have that advantage but we do have the only thing on earth that has any chance of producing hard evidence.

If Thomas were here today he would likely be living by the same rules: not believing unless he can see and touch for himself. Now the information on the shroud has been gathered and it is time for Thomas to make decisions: painting, natural phenomenon, or wonder that remains unexplained and finally if it is the latter, is this Jesus' shroud, and is there any evidence for resurrection?

Starting with the blood marks, Thomas has the chemistry results that tell him it is real blood and, more important to someone who has to see for himself, he has the forensic study that concurs that the cloth covered the body of a man who was crucified. There are also the wounds that are identical to those inflicted upon Jesus even down to the minute details such as the flow of "blood and water."[1] He could see also that the scourging was done by an instrument that caused wounds that could have been inflicted by a first century Roman flagrum. With this visual information at hand that he could reproduce, it is probably safe to admit that Thomas would say: Yes, a crucified man who died like Jesus, was buried in this cloth, but was it Jesus? Yes, these blood marks are a natural phenomena.

Thomas of today would also want to know as much as he could about the image and how it was made. Now he would look at the scientific literature and find that 99 percent of scientists worldwide who have studied the cloth up close, using the latest technical instruments, have found that it is not a painting. Furthermore, the process causing the yellowness of the topmost fibers of the threads responsible for the image is unknown. The shading quality of the image is more like the results of modern printing technology. These scientists say they do not know how the image was made. But Thomas, having specific rules that he lives by would not necessarily believe these witnesses because he has not seen for himself. So he would turn to the shroud micrographs and look carefully for the residue of paint or powder. He may then leave the micrographs, still not certain about the evidence, and turn to the larger pictures asking if this image was formed by the same contact mechanism that caused the blood marks on the cloth.

After turning to the studies of the blood off the left elbow and blood on the face, he would see for himself that if the image were created by contact, it would be grotesque with the back of the upper arm showing and the sides of the face would be out to where the blood marks are in the hair. This would convince him that the image is not caused by cloth touching the perspiration and organic matter on a body. The image is not a contact process. He would then turn back to the shroud micrographs and possibly be satisfied that it was not a painting.

So he is left with only one alternative, to see if anyone else has made such a complex image with photographic, three dimensional and x-ray-like qualities. If found, he must explore that image at the microscopic level to see if it compares with the specifics found on the shroud fibers.

He finds an occasional scientist who says it is a painting but each time he checks one of the claims based on attempted reproductions he finds that the paint, no matter how fine, has either soaked to the back of the cloth, or that the powder is seen in between the fibers and does not look at all like the micrographs of the shroud.

He then presented his case to a group of scientists who are convinced as he is that there was a crucified man under this cloth, but they conclude that someone painted the image using some unknown technique that deteriorated over the years and left the negative image that we see. He thought about that and at first was turned on to the idea, then asked the scientific group to show him the evidence. They said, That technique may have been lost; we cannot do that. With that, Thomas was understandably confused, but for only a few minutes. He looked at them and said, This is pure speculation. I do not believe you, and I will not believe you until you show me a reproduction of the shroud with its complex image and its yellowed fibers just as we find on the shroud.

So looking back and seeing that no one has come up with any explanation and reproduction either man made or natural in the last 100 years, Thomas would likely feel confident to conclude at this time, that the image on the shroud can be considered without any doubt a wonder that remains unexplained.

Now it is time to ask Thomas, Is this the shroud of Jesus and does it give us any evidence for the resurrection? These are good questions to ask Thomas, a Jew of the first century, and a man who would know the customs of his countrymen. He also walked with and listened to Jesus' every word.

First, in looking at the blood marks, Thomas' discerning eye would see that the blood clots on the cloth are undisturbed. That means that whoever took this man down from the position of crucifixion took great care to be sure that the blood clots were not disturbed. This information would make him very suspicious that this was a Jewish burial. Why, because he knows his countrymen would be concerned about the mingled blood, the life blood that was on this man when they took the body down from the cross, and that they would take great care not to disturb it.

Thomas would then be given access to the Whanger-Danin study of faint flower images seen on the cloth and would recognize that all of them come from his country, flowers he may have picked as a child. And most striking to him is that he would recall that these plants bloom in the spring at Passover time, the same time that Jesus was crucified and buried. Unfortunately, he could not confirm that they put flowers on his shroud because at the time he was frightened and in hiding and never saw the crucifixion or the burial.

Finally it is pointed out to Thomas that there are what appear to be shadows on the body image, that the hair falls down to the shoulders and the soles of the feet are seen on the shroud. Thomas looks at the shroud and sees that this image, in contrast to the blood marks, is not that of a man lying down. He gazes at this upright image, at this man who was laid out in death with closed eyes, fatal wounds, stiffened arms and legs and flesh[2], and sees that this dead man has been lifted from the position of burial and is now upright as if suspended in midair.

Thomas would move back from this image in awe because Thomas knows something that most of us do not know unless we read the gospels. He was with Jesus and heard his every word. Many times in the gospels it is said that the Father would raise him. Thomas heard Jesus say, "And I, when I am lifted up from the earth, will draw all people to myself"* (John 12:32).[3] Now before him on the shroud is the very same imagery that Jesus talked about some 2000 years ago—the raised Jesus, the Jesus who

---

* Raymond Brown and others believe that "being lifted up" includes Jesus' being lifted in crucifixion, resurrection, and ascension.

is lifted up from the earth. This image is not that of Jesus lying in burial. It is not a static motionless image of death but is dynamic and moving. Jesus had been lifted from his position of burial by the Father, lifted up above the earth. This was the profound event that no one ever saw. Yes, this is Jesus' shroud and this image is the reflection of the moment of his resurrection.

I stopped to consider Thomas' response to the image of the upright man. At the same time I thought about Alan Adler and our discussion about the shroud. Adler is right. There is no scientific test for telling us that this is Jesus. (Only if one had a sample of Jesus' blood, then one could conceivably see if there is a DNA match with the blood on the shroud; but that is not possible.) Science can only do so much, and so far, it tells us that this image is a wonder that remains unexplained. But there is much more than science to be considered here. How can we expect to understand this image unless we look to the Word of God as Thomas has?

Remember Thomas—question everything—learn for yourself.

Now Thomas and his friends experienced an event that is very pertinent to our discussion about the shroud image and the resurrection. Specifically, I am referring to Jesus after the resurrection, and to the time he appeared to the disciples in the locked house. Jesus is described as having come and stood among them although the doors were locked—fascinating story and something that we have never experienced. Whether you believe it to be or not, it is worth pursuing. Why? Because this story, along with a few other stories, gives us the only information that we have about the resurrected Jesus. If we examine the physics of the event, it tells us that Jesus did not follow our ordinary under-standing of space and time.[4] Now let us be very specific here. When I walk from one side of the room to another, I move through the space (height, width, depth) of that room and it takes a certain amount of time to cross the room depending on how fast I walk. Jesus did neither. He just showed up in their midst ignoring our understanding of space and time.

Incredible as this seems, we have a parallel to this very same kind of experience when we look at the shroud—most specifically, the difficulty of understanding image formation. Remember the experiment of placing a cloth napkin over your face. Here we discovered that image formation on the shroud does not follow our ordinary understanding of space and time. How would Thomas compare the moment of image formation to the moment when Jesus appeared in front of him? From his perspective, he had the advantage of seeing Jesus appear in the middle of a room. Now we are allowing Thomas the opportunity to join us and look at and participate in an experiment which fulfills his criteria of seeing and touching. There is little doubt that he would agree that both events have something very important in common—they both fall outside our ordinary understanding of time and space.

In the general run of life, there are few things that fall outside the experience of the world that we live in—the world of the four dimensions of height, width, depth, and time. This is our home, our universe and it is all we know. But all of a sudden there are two events, one you can see and feel and the other is directly connected to the first but is something you and I have never seen. It comes down to us from witnesses that saw this event almost 2000 years ago. And now at this time, they come together. One we see and touch: The Thomas rule intact. One we never saw, but Thomas did: The Thomas report.

After Thomas looked at the data and became familiar with how we look at the world today from the point of view of the four dimensions, he was moved by the whole experience. Again he had the advantage of being there and knowing the words of Jesus. Now for the first time he began to better understand some of the language that Jesus used which he had previously thought about but from a different point of view.

Thomas went on to explain that since he was able to look at the modern world and learn something about our new technology and space travel, he was starting to look at the earth, stars, and the universe, our world from a different perspective. He could see that there was no heaven up there in space. At first that disappointed him greatly but now he was no longer concerned. The truth about heaven, if you wish to call it that, was gradually becoming clear. This new experience with the shroud image and his previous experience with Jesus in the locked house was starting to help him focus on what Jesus was talking about when he would say: "I come from the Father and have come into the world and am going to the Father" (Jn 16:20). Or "If I have told you about earthly things and you do not believe, how can you believe if I tell you about heavenly things? No one has ascended into heaven except the one who descended from heaven, the Son of Man" (Jn 3:12-13).

Now from Thomas' perspective, it was starting to become clear that Jesus was again talking figuratively to make a point as he often did in his teaching. Heaven was not up in the sky but Jesus was using those terms of ascending and descending to give that imagery so that the old world that Thomas was from could better understand that Jesus was from a special place. Now it was becoming clear to Thomas that this place was indeed not of this world, our universe, but was totally apart from the four dimensions of our ordinary experience.

I thought about Thomas' perspective and it reminded me of a recent event that I attended at the Wang theater in Boston in October of 1999. My son and I and many of his friends attended a lecture by Stephen Hawking, author of *A Brief History of Time*.[5] After his lecture he answered a number of questions, and I recall the very first question and answer paraphrased here: "What was it like one moment before the big bang?" His answer: "We don't know, it remains undefined." In other words, in this one moment—the moment before our universe, our world of four dimensions (height, width, depth, and time)—this one moment before the big bang remains undefined. Our understanding of space and time breaks down at the big bang and at any events before it; therefore, our understanding of space and time cannot be used to define this one moment.[6] Two other situations come to mind, the result of one is the shroud image that we can still see and touch. The other is one that we have heard about for 2000 years —Thomas' experience in the locked house. These three situations, the moment before the big bang, the moment of the creation of the shroud image, and the moment of the appearance of Jesus in a locked room all have in common the fact that they cannot be defined by our ordinary under-standing of space and time.

After contemplating this, I went to the Gospel of John to check on something I recalled from my boyhood; Jesus' response to one of Pilate's questions on that fateful day almost 2000 years ago: "What have you done?" Jesus began his answer with, "My kingdom is not from this world." (John 18:35-36.) I now looked upon these words from an entirely new perspective. Did Pilate really understand what Jesus meant, or is it only now in our scientific age that we can really understand what Jesus meant by "not from this world", not of our world of time and space.

Now when I look at the complex image of the shroud with its mixture of photographic, X-ray like and three dimensional qualities, I wonder why I had been trying so long to comprehend how the image got onto the cloth that wrapped this crucified man? Imagine getting an image such as this from a sheet that is draped over a body! Something awesome that we barely have begun to understand happened to this cloth. From where did this complex image come?

For whom was it created? Only for today's two billion Christians? I do not think so. Rather that we ponder this image and ask if this is the manifestation of the power of our Creator over death—death our own personal nemesis which is a certainty regardless of any medical advances. Is this image God's message—eternal life offered to every person who has, does and will live on this earth? After twenty years of critical research I am now convinced that this image is indeed God's message: "And I, when I am lifted up from the earth, will draw all people to myself." (John 12:32)[7]

Remember Thomas, question everything, think for yourself.

Thomas was at another event that marked the beginning of the human drama which eventually concluded with the resurrection. It was the last supper. There was a small group of Jewish people celebrating the Passover meal and toward the end Jesus first offered them a piece of bread as his body and then a cup of wine as his blood.

Neither I nor anyone else can tell you what was on the minds of the apostles when Jesus did this. Only from the discussion on Jewish burial customs do we know that a quarter log of blood is the contents of one and one half eggs, about the volume of a small cup of wine. When spilled at the time of death, this quantity of blood is the necessary amount to be considered life-blood—the blood of atonement. These men knew that. They also knew that it was forbidden to eat blood. From the Torah, they knew that, "If anyone of the house of Israel or of the aliens who reside among them eats any blood, I will set my face against that person who eats blood, and will cut that person off from the people." (Leviticus 17:10) Never mind drinking life blood—eating any blood was forbidden by God. By participating in this ceremony, unless they were certain that Jesus was the Messiah, they were partaking in an act that was forbidden, that was blasphemous. If discovered by their countrymen, they would be cut off from their people and may even lose their very lives.

Now again we do not have any statement that tells us what was on their minds that night. But we do know what happened in the next few days that helps us to understand what they may have been thinking. First, we know that Judas continued with his plan of betrayal. Second, we know that on three occasions on that very night, Peter denied ever knowing Jesus. Third, we know that on the Mount of Olives the apostles ran in fear of their lives and deserted Jesus. Fourth, after the crucifixion, we find these men, all Jews, living in a locked house hiding in fear of the Jewish authority. Lies, secrecy, living in hiding became the way of life for this small group once Jesus was gone.

Why shouldn't they be in fear of their countrymen? If any had believed that Jesus was the Messiah at the last supper, that belief was now gone for Jesus had just died a humiliating death on a cross. They now sat in that locked house thinking they had participated in a ceremony forbidden by God. The followers of Jesus were not only living in fear of their lives but they were filled with guilt. No one in that house was about to even whisper Jesus' name, let alone tell the world about the preacher of love, faith and hope. In the end, no one would ever know that Jesus the carpenter was born. But something happened in that house that changed the hearts and minds of those men—changed despair to hope, fear of death to virtually no fear of death. An event that caused them to write down the details of the experience with no premonition or understanding of what it would mean in the future. In spite of locked doors, Jesus appeared in their midst— joyfully they watched as he stood among them—such an incredible story.

So fragile was their story that Thomas who was not there would not believe a word of it. "Unless I see the marks of the nails in his hands and put my finger in the marks of the nails and my hand in his side, I will not believe." (John 20:25) Think about Thomas as he entered the house. He likely just stepped out of the shadows of an alley for fear that he would be recognized. He might be carrying food for his small group but more important as he entered he would be burdened not only by fear but by the guilt of knowing he disobeyed God. He hears their story as soon as they shut and lock the door behind him. Who would believe such a story? In anger he makes his famous retort. Thomas, a man ahead of his time, a true scientist who wants proof, is a man who in the end got his proof and was brought to believe.

The report of Thomas and that of the other witnesses was enough. Two thousand years later Jesus has two billion followers. Obviously without the resurrection, we would all be reading a different history book.

After two millennia of struggling to increase our knowledge we have come this far and are beginning to grasp our universe: to understand the four dimensions that we exist in and to know that there was a moment before the big bang that remains undefined, a moment that cannot be defined by our ordinary understanding of space and time. Is the shroud image here to give us a glimpse of a moment that cannot be defined by our ordinary understanding of space and time? Perhaps this experience with the shroud image may bring us back to a locked house where a small group of men, living in fear for their very existence, were eventually vindicated by the appearance of the resurrected Jesus who is no longer constrained by space and time. Perhaps the shroud image has survived to enable a modern world to share the same boundless joy that a small group of desperate men felt 2,000 years ago.

Notes and References

Chapter One
A PHYSICIAN'S PERSPECTIVE

1. Gary Habermas, *The Historical Jesus* (Missouri: College Press Publishing Co., Inc., 1982).
2. Pierre Barbet, *A Doctor at Calvary* (New York: Doubleday and Co., Inc., 1953).
3. In 1983, the House of Savoy willed the shroud to the Roman Catholic Church. The shroud remains in Turin Cathedral where it has been kept since 1578.
4. Barbet, 6–7.
5. Ian Wilson, *The Shroud of Turin* (New York: Doubleday and Co., Inc., 1978), 13–14.
6. Barbet, 17.
7. Ibid., 17.
8. Ibid., 31.
9. Ibid., 17.
10. Ibid., 91. Multiple facial wounds described by Barbet.
11. Ibid., 92.
12. Ibid., 92.
13. Ibid., 93–97.
14. Ibid., 129–147.
15. Ibid., 121–128.
16. Ibid., 148–152.

17. Ibid., 107.
18. Ibid., 103 and 124. There are some early examples of art forms showing the nail through the wrist. The most famous is the Gero Crucifix of Cologne from the tenth century. (Personal communication with Dorothy Crispino.)
19. Ibid., 110–112.
20. Ibid., 118.
21. Ibid., 119.

Chapter Two
BECOMING PARTICIPANTS

1. Pierre Barbet, *A Doctor at Calvary* (New York: Doubleday and Co., 1953), 8.
2. Ibid., 32.

Chapter Three
NOT MADE BY HUMAN HANDS

1. Max Frei, "Nine Years of Palinological Studies on the Shroud," *Shroud Spectrum International* (June 1982): 3. (English spelling is Palynological.)
2. Ibid., 5.
3. Ibid., 5–7.
4. Ibid., 7.
5. Ian Wilson, *The Shroud of Turin* (New York: Doubleday and Co., Inc., 1978), 116.
6. Edward Gibbon, *The Decline and Fall of the Roman Empire,* vol. II (Chicago: Encyclopedia Britannica, Inc., 1952), 196–197.
7. IanWilson, *The Blood and the Shroud* (New York: Touchstone, 1998), 268.
8. IanWilson, *The Shroud of Turin* (New York: Doubleday and Co., Inc., 1978), 145.
9. Ibid., 147.
10. Ibid., 145–147.
11. Ibid., chapter 20, 165–183.

12. Ian Wilson, The Shroud of Turin (New York: Doubleday and Co., Inc., 1978) *The Blood and the Shroud* (New York: Touchstone, 1998).

13. John Jackson, Eric Jumper, and William Ercoline, "Correlation of Image Intensity on the Turin Shroud with the 3-D Structure of a Human Body Shape," *Applied Optics,* vol. 23 (July 15, 1984): 2247.

14. Ibid., 2249.

15. A. Whanger and M. Whanger, *The Shroud of Turin* (Franklin, Tennessee: Providence House Publishers, 1998),111.

16. Among the outstanding American scientific literature that is presently available on the shroud are the following, which are very technical:

   a. L.A. Schwalbe and R.N. Rogers, "Physics and Chemistry of the Shroud of Turin: A Summary of the 1978 Investigation," *Analytica Chimica Acta,* vol. 135 (1982): 3–49.

   b. J.H. Heller and A.D. Adler, "A Chemical Investigation of the Shroud of Turin," *Canadian Society of Forensic Science Journal,* vol. 14, no. 3 (1981): 81–103.

   c. V.D. Miller and S.F. Pellicori, "Ultraviolet Fluorescence Photography of the Shroud of Turin," *Journal of Biological Photography,* vol. 49, no. 3 (July 1981): 71–85.

   d. S.F. Pellicori and R.A. Chandos, "Portable Unit Permits UV/Vis Study of Shroud," *Industrial Research and Development* (February 1981): 186–189.

   e. R.A. Morris, L.A. Schwalbe, and J.R. London, "X-Ray Fluorescence Investigation of the Shroud of Turin," *X-Ray Spectrometry,* vol. 9, no. 2 (1980): 40–47.

   f. J.H. Heller and A.D. Adler, "Blood on the Shroud of Turin," *Applied Optics,* vol. 19, no. 16 (August 15, 1980): 2742–2744.

   g. E.J. Jumper and R.W. Mottern, "Scientific Investigation of the Shroud of Turin," *Applied Optics* (June 15, 1980): 1909–1912.

   h. S.F. Pellicori, "Spectral Properties of the Shroud of Turin," *Applied Optics* (June 15, 1980): 1913–1920.

i. J.S. Accetta and J.S. Baumgart, "Infrared Reflectance Spectroscopy and Thermographic Investigations of the Shroud of Turin," *Applied Optics* (June 15, 1980): 1921–1929.

j. Roger Gilbert and Marion Gilbert, "Ultraviolet-Visible Reflectance and Fluorescence Spectra of the Shroud of Turin," *Applied Optics* (June 15, 1980): 1930–1936.

k. R.W. Mottern, R.J. London, and R.A. Morris, "Radiographic Examination of the Shroud of Turin—A Preliminary Report," *Materials Evaluation,* vol. 38, no. 12 (1979): 39–44.

l. V. Miller and D. Lynn, "De Lijkwada Van Turijn," *Natuur en Techniek* (February 1981): 102–125.

m. Robert Bucklin, "The Shroud of Turin: A Pathologist's Viewpoint," *Legal Medicine Annual* (1981).

n. S. Pellicori and M. Evans, "The Shroud of Turin Through the Microscope," *Archaeology* (January–February 1981): 32–42.

17. Schwalbe and Rogers, "Physics and Chemistry of the Shroud of Turin," op. cit., 31. "There has been no evidence found to suggest that the visible image results from a colored foreign material on the cloth. In this regard, the data are quite internally consistent. Microscopic studies have revealed the image to be highly superficial; the image resides in the topmost fibers of the woven material as a translucent yellow discoloration. No pigment particles can be resolved by direct Shroud observation at 50x magnification, nor can unambiguously identified pigment particles be found on the tape samples at 1,000x. Microchemical studies of yellow fibrils taken from tape samples of the pure-image area have shown no indication for the presence of dyes, stains, inorganic pigments, or protein-, starch-, or wax-based painting media. X-ray fluorescence shows no detectable difference in elemental composition between image and non-image areas. Spectrophotometric reflectance reveals none of the characteristic spectral features of pigments or dyes. Ultraviolet fluorescence shows no indication of aromatic

dyes or aromatic amino acids that might be expected from animal-collagen pigment binders. Direct visual observations of image areas that intersect scorch and water stains reveal nothing that might suggest the presence of organic dyes or water- protein-, or starch-based painting media."

18. McCrone's four articles:

   a. Walter C. McCrone and C. Skirius, "Light Microscopical Study of the Turin 'Shroud' I," *The Microscope,* vol. 28, no. 3 (1980): 105–113.

   b. Walter C. McCrone, "Light Microscopical Study of the Turin 'Shroud' II," *The Microscope,* vol. 28, no. 4 (1980): 115–128.

   c. Walter C. McCrone, "Microscopical Study of the Turin 'Shroud' III," *The Microscope,* vol. 29 (1981): 19–39.

   d. Walter C. McCrone, "The Shroud of Turin: Blood or Artist's Pigment?" *Accounts of Chemical Research,* vol. 23, no. 3 (1990): 77–87.

19. Scientific reviews of McCrone's articles:

   a. Pellicori and Evans, "The Shroud of Turin through the Microscope," op. cit., 42.

   b. Schwalbe and Rogers, "Physics and Chemistry of the Shroud of Turin," op. cit., 11–16.

   c. Jackson, Jumper, and Ercoline, "Correlation of Image Intensity on the Turin Shroud with the 3-D Structure of a Human Body Shape," op. cit., 2251–2253.

   d. Eric Jumper, Alan Adler, John Jackson, Samuel Pellicori, John Heller, and James Druzik, "A Comprehensive Examination of the Various Stains and Images on the Shroud of Turin," *Archaeological Chemistry III,* edited by J. Lambert, ACS Advances in Chemistry, no. 205 (1984): 447–476.

   e. Heller and Adler, "A Chemical Investigation of the Shroud of Turin," op. cit., 81–103.

   f. Personal communication from Jumper and Adler concerning article "17-d," p. 468: "Under the experimental conditions employed in the x-ray investigation on the shroud, unfortunately iron would not be expected to show images as was implied in the review article. However, vermilion (mercuric sulfide, HgS) would be seen."

   g. For the reader who is scientifically inclined, I would suggest carefully reading McCrone's article "16-d," Adler's article "17-e," and Jumper's article "17-d" so that you may decide for yourself, at the microscopic and chemical level, whether or not the shroud is a painting. To fully comprehend McCrone's article, you need to review the colored pictures in his article.

20. Heller and Adler, "Blood on the Shroud of Turin," op. cit., 2742. For those interested in reading more about the blood on the shroud, I suggest reading the work of Pierluigi Baima Bollone. His own bibliography is in his *Shroud Spectrum International* articles. See bibliography.

21. Heller and Adler, "A Chemical Investigation of the Shroud of Turin," op. cit., 81.

22. Among Adler's best articles are the following:
   a. Heller and Adler, "A Chemical Investigation of the Shroud of Turin," op. cit.
   b. Heller and Adler, "Blood on the Shroud of Turin," op. cit.
   c. Jumper, Adler, et al., "A Comprehensive Examination of the Various Stains and Images on the Shroud of Turin," op. cit.

23. Schwalbe and Rogers, "Physics and Chemistry of the Shroud of Turin," op. cit., 36.

24. Pellicori and Evans, "The Shroud of Turin through the Microscope," op. cit., 41.

25. Schwalbe and Rogers, "Physics and Chemistry of the Shroud of Turin," op. cit., 11.

26. Heller and Adler, "A Chemical Investigation of the Shroud of Turin," op. cit., 81. "There is no chemical evidence for the application of any pigments, stains, or dyes on the cloth to produce the

image found thereon. The chemical differences between image and non-image areas of the cloth indicate that the image was produced by some dehydrative oxidative process of the cellulose structure of the linen to yield a conjugated carbonyl group as the chromophore. However, a detailed mechanism for the production of this image, accounting for all of its properties, remains undetermined."

27. Articles describing the use of substances to produce yellowing of fibers are the following:
    a. Heller and Adler, "A Chemical Investigation of the Shroud of Turin," op. cit., 98–99.
    b. Pellicori, "Spectral Properties of the Shroud of Turin," op. cit., 1913–1920.

28. Four of the best articles describing the problems of the contact theory are the following:
    a. Schwalbe and Rogers, "Physics and Chemistry of the Shroud of Turin," op. cit., 35. "If the image had been caused by the catalytic action of materials present on the corpse, direct contact of the body with the cloth seems to be the only likely material transfer mechanism. A general problem now becomes apparent. It would seem to follow that the dorsal image area was influenced by the weight of the body whereas the frontal image was imprinted only by the lesser weight of the covering cloth. Recall, however, that the densities at presumed contact points on both frontal and dorsal images do not differ significantly. These characteristics along with the superficial nature of the image would suggest that the contact transfer mechanism is pressure-independent. This apparent contradiction challenges not only the Pellicori-German model but most other hypotheses in this category."
    b. Pellicori and Evans, "The Shroud of Turin through the Microscope," op. cit., 43.
    c. Heller and Adler, "A Chemical Investigation of the Shroud of Turin," op. cit., 98–99

d. Jumper, Adler, et. al., "A Comprehensive Examination of the Various Stains and Images on the Shroud of Turin," op. cit., 470. "The Shroud's mapping relationship, however, poses the strongest objection to a contact mechanism. Contact mechanisms have not been able to produce a convincing cloth-body distance relationship. In fact, taken alone, this mapping function seems to suggest some kind of a "projection" mechanism, because there seems to be image present even where it does not appear to have been possible that the cloth was in contact with the body. We are left to identify what kind of 'projection' mechanism, and this we have been unable to do. Simple molecular diffusion and 'radiation' models, for example, fail to account for the apparent resolution of the image as we understand it."

29. Jackson, Jumper, and Ercoline, "Correlation of Image Intensity on the Turin Shroud with the 3-D Structure of a Human Body Shape" op. cit., 2244–2270.

30. No mechanism is known that will reproduce the body-to-cloth transfer. The following articles discuss this:
    a. Ibid.
    b. Schwalbe and Rogers, "Physics and Chemistry of the Shroud of Turin," op.cit., 35.
    c. Heller and Adler, "A Chemical Investigation of the Shroud of Turin," op. cit., 99.

31. Jumper, Adler, et. al., "A Comprehensive Examination of the Various Stains and Images on the Shroud of Turin," op. cit., 460.

32. Ibid., 447–476.

33. Ibid., 450–451, and verbal communication with Jumper regarding wicking.

34. Ibid., 450 and 459.

35. Pellicori and Evans, "The Shroud of Turin through the Microscope," op. cit., 41. (*Personal communication with Jumper:* The image fibers penetrated the thread one fiber deep and possibly

in some places, two fibers deep, even though it says three to four fibers deep on page 41 of Pellicori's article.)

36. Jumper, Adler, et. al., "A Comprehensive Examination of the Various Stains and Images on the Shroud of Turin," op. cit., 451.

37. P.E. Damon, D.J. Donahue, B.H. Gore, et. al, "Radiocarbon Dating of the Shroud of Turin," *Nature*, vol. 337 (February 16, 1989): 611-615.

38. A Danin, A. Whanger, U. Baruch, et. al., *Flora of the Shroud of Turin*, (Missouri Botanical Garden Press, 1999), 24.

39. New information on radiocarbon dating:
   a. G. Harbottle and W. Heino, "Carbon Dating the Shroud of Turin," *Archaeological Chemistry*-IV: Allen, R.O., ed.: Advances in Chemistry, no. 220; American Chemical Society (1989): 313-320.
   b. A.D. Adler, "Updating Recent Studies on the Shroud of Turin," *Archaeological Chemistry*: Orna, M.V., ed.: ACS Symposium Series, no. 625 (1996): 223-228.
   c. M.V. Orna, "Doing Chemistry at the Art/Archaeology Interface," *Journal of Chemical Education*, vol. 74, no. 3 (April 1997): 373-376.

40. Harbottle, 318-319.

41. Adler, 225.

42. Harbottle, 316.

43. Adler, 225.

44. Orna, 375.

45. For further discussion, these references are recommended:
   a. Harbottle, 313-320.
   b. Adler, 223-228.
   c. Orna, 373-376.

Chapter Four
JEWISH BURIAL CUSTOMS

1. *The Mishnah,* translated by Herbert Danby. (Oxford: Oxford University Press, 1933), Second Division, Moed. Tractate: Shabbath, 23[5], 120.

2. Maurice Lamm, *The Jewish Way in Death and Mourning* (New York: Jonathan David, Publishers, 1969), 6–7.

3. Ibid., 244.

4. Solomon Ganzfried, *Code of Jewish Law (Kitzur Shulchan Aruch),* translated by Hyman E. Goldin (New York: Hebrew Publishing Company, 1963) vol. IV, ch. 197. *The Purification, Shrouds, and Utilization of Anything Belonging to the Dead* (Tahara), nos. 9 and 10, 99–100.

5. *The Mishnah,* op.cit., Introduction, XIII.

6. *The Mishnah,* op.cit., Third Division, Nashim. Tractate: Nazir, 7[2], 289–290.

7. Ibid., Sixth Division, Tohoroth. Tractate: Oholoth, 3[5], 653–654.

8. Ibid., Appendix II: Money, Weights, and Measures, 798.

9. Ibid., Third Division, Nashim. Tractate: Nazir, 7[2], 290.

10. Ganzfried, *Code of Jewish Law,* op. cit., 99.

11. Ibid., 100.

12. *The Mishnah,* op.cit., Fifth Division, Kodashim. Tractate: Zebahim, 3[1], note. 4, 471.

13. Bonnie Lavoie, Gilbert Lavoie, Daniel Klutstein, and John Regan, "In Accordance with Jewish Burial Custom, the Body of Jesus Was Not Washed," *Sindon* (December 1981): 19–29. Also in *Shroud Spectrum International* (June 1982): 8–17 and *Biblical Archeologist,* "Polemics and Irenics" (Winter 1981): 5–6.

Chapter Five
A CRUCIFIED MAN

1. *The Mishnah,* translated by Herbert Danby. (Oxford: Oxford University Press, 1933), Sixth Division, Tohoroth, Tractate: Oholoth, 3[5], 654.

2. Gilbert Lavoie, Bonnie Lavoie, Vincent Donovan, and John Ballas, "Blood on the Shroud of Turin: Part I," *Shroud Spectrum International* (June 1983): 15–19.

Chapter Six
BLOOD TRANSFERS TO CLOTH

1. Gilbert Lavoie, Bonnie Lavoie, Vincent Donovan, and John Ballas, "Blood on the Shroud of Turin: Part II," *Shroud Spectrum International,* no. 8 (1983): 2–10.
2. Clara Davidsohn and Minnie Wells, Todd-Sanford Clinical Diagnosis by Laboratory Methods. Philadelphia: W.B. Saunders Co. (1962): 346.
3. Ibid., 332.
4. Ibid., 330.
5. I placed three drops of normal saline on all of the clots fifteen minutes prior to each of the half-hour sample times throughout the four-hour period. However, once the cloth was placed on a clot, no further saline was placed on that clot.
6. Pierre Barbet, *A Doctor at Calvary* (New York: Doubleday and Co. Inc., 1953, Appendix I.) According to Barbet's description of the death of a man hung by his arms, profuse sweat pours from the body just prior to the time of death.
7. *The Mishnah,* translated by Herbert Danby. (Oxford: Oxford University Press, 1933), Second Division, Moed. Tractate: Shabbath, 23⁵, 120.
8. The 1995 Israeli Calendar, published by the Government Press Office, Jerusalem, Israel, obtained from the Israeli Consulate, Boston, Massachusetts.
9. Vern Miller and S. F. Pellicori, "Ultraviolet Fluorescence Photography of the Shroud of Turin," *Journal of Biological Photography,* vol. 49, no. 3 (July 1981): 75.
10. Ibid., 82.
11. J.H. Heller and A.D. Adler, "A Chemical Investigation of the Shroud of Turin," *Canadian Society of Forensic Science Journal,* vol. 14, no. 3 (1981): 96.
12. *The Mishnah,* op. cit., Sixth Division, Tohoroth. Tractate: Oholoth, 3⁵, 653–654.
13. Barbet, op. cit., 24–25.

Chapter Seven
BEYOND OUR UNDERSTANDING OF SPACE AND TIME

1. Pierre Barbet, *A Doctor at Calvary* (New York: Doubleday and Co., Inc., 1953): 32.
2. Gilbert Lavoie, Bonnie Lavoie, and Alan Adler, "Blood on the Shroud of Turin: Part III, The Blood on the Face," *Shroud Spectrum International* (September 1986): 3–6.

Chapter Eight
THE UPRIGHT MAN

1. The hair of the shroud image has a three dimensional quality by VP8 image analysis (Unpublished VP8 Image Study done by G.R. Lavoie, M.D. and Kevin Moran in the 1990's)
2. Some of the contents of Chapter 8 were presented at the 1989 Paris International Shroud Symposium.

Chapter Nine
THE THOMAS REPORT

1. From a medical point of view, the source of the blood could have been from the large vessels of the chest or from the heart. The source of the water could have been from pleural fluid (that can look like water), which accumulated in the chest cavity. The causes of fluid accumulation in the chest are numerous. A plausible cause may have been congestive heart failure, which could have resulted from shock (blood and fluid loss, causing a profound drop in blood pressure leading to death). No one can know the exact mechanisms of the occurrence but the flow of "blood and water" is certainly medically possible.

On the back image of the shroud, along the waist, there is a large liquidlike flow (Figure 1). This flow consists of several streams of what appears to be bloody fluid (blood mixed with a lighter clearer fluid) that flow beyond the perimeter of the body image. The blood marks that reach beyond the body image are located below the paralleling patches where the burns occurred during the fire of 1532. The water marks that quenched the smol-

dering linen at that time are located around the patches and inter-
mingle with the blood marks. These water marks seen on each side
of the body are surrounded by a very light line that determines
their perimeters.* On close observation of the streams at the small
of the back (Figure 1), there are light, nearly colorless areas of fluid
interspersed between the darker areas of blood, reminiscent of the
flow of "blood and water" described in the Gospel of John.

Figure 1

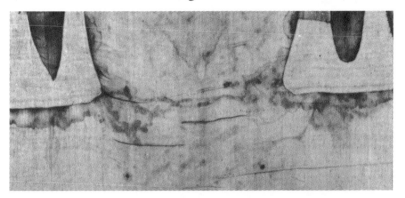

Figure 2

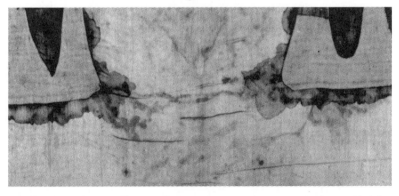

* The water marks are better seen in Figure 2 where the gray area has been added for
clarity. The outer perimeters on the gray zones in Figure 2 demonstrate the outer
perimeter of the water marks. When looking at Vern Miller's full-size high resolution
colored photograph, one can more easily distinguish between the blood and the
lighter clearer fluid, the water marks, and the burn marks. (Technical support for this
study supplied by Kevin Moran and Andre Lavoie.)

Again, like the flow of "blood and water," no one knows the specific circumstances causing the flow across the lower back, but some reasonable assumptions as to the major events leading up to this formation can be made. Very likely, this flow of bloody fluid came from the open side-wound after the body was taken down from the vertical position of crucifixion and placed on the shroud in the horizontal position in preparation for burial. The blood and fluid flowed down the side of the chest onto the shroud. It then flowed behind the small of the back and across to the opposite side of the back and beyond. (Years ago, a similar flow of fluid from the chest to the back was reproduced by Vernon Miller and his team. *Verbal communication with Vernon Miller.*)

When considering the blood marks of the shroud, John's description of Jesus' death is exact, even down to the detail of the flow of "blood and water." Indeed, with the shroud in hand, there is no doubt of John's accuracy: "His testimony is true, and he knows that he tells the truth" (19:35).

2. Personal communication with Alan Adler—He states that the lower backside appears flattened per the VP8 image analyser. In rechecking this area, I also noted that the scourge marks at the middle area of the lower backside, especially toward the right (Figure 13 of Chapter 8), do suggest the possibility of a flattened lower backside. (The flatness of a body part can be best appreciated by placing the calf of one's leg on a glass table and observing the flatness from under the table. However, the type of flattening that is seen in the autopsy room, caused by the subject lying on a hard surface, continues to persist even after the body is lifted up from a hard surface table.)

The observation of a possible partial flattening of the lower backside of the shroud image would be consistent with the corpse having been laid in the supine position on a hard surface. This observation is the logical consequence of other findings: chest wound, scourged body, wounds of crucifixion—all contributing causes leading to death. However, among these findings are what look like shadows under the lower backside (see Figure 1C of Chapter 1) and under the hair (compare Figure 10 to 11B of Chapter 8) as well as the flow of hair down to the shoulders and upper back. These observations are consistent with an image of an upright man.

3. Information on the Raised and Lifted Jesus

    a. Raymond Brown, *The Virginal Conception and Bodily Resurrection of Jesus* (New York: Paulist Press, 1973) 78-80.

    b. Raymond Brown, *The Gospel According to John*, vol. 29 (I-XII) and vol. 29A (XIII-XXI) (New York: Doubleday and Co., Inc., 1986), CXV in introduction.

    c. Ibid., 146.

4. Raymond Brown, *The Virginal Conception and Bodily Resurrection of Jesus* (New York: Paulist Press, 1973) 111.

5. Stephen Hawking, *A Brief History of Time* (New York: Bantam Books, 1998).

6. Ibid., 126. "At the singularity [the big bang], general relativity and all other physical laws would break down: one couldn't predict what would come out of the singularity. As explained before, this means that one might as well cut the big bang, and any events before it, out of the theory, because they can have no effect on what we observe. Space-time *would* have a boundary – a beginning at the big bang.

7. Raymond Brown, *The Gospel According to John*, vol. 29 (I-XII) and vol. 29A (XIII-XXI) (New York: Doubleday and Co., Inc., 1986), 146.

Bibliography

Accetta, J. and J.S. Baumgart. "Infrared Reflectance Spectroscopy and Thermographic Investigations of the Shroud of Turin." *Applied Optics* (June 15, 1980): 1921–1929.

Adler, Alan. "Updating Recent Studies on the Shroud of Turin." *Archaeological Chemistry:* M. V. Orna, ed., ACS Symposium Series, no. 625 (1996): 223–228.

Barbet, Pierre. *A Doctor at Calvary.* New York: Doubleday and Co., Inc., 1953.

Beasley-Murray, George R. *Word Biblical Commentary.* Volume II. John. Waco, Texas: Word Books, 1987.

Bollone, Pierluigi Baima, M. Jorio, and A.L. Massaro. "Identification of the Group of the Traces of Human Blood on the Shroud." *Shroud Spectrum International.* (March 1983): 3–6.

Bollone, Pierluigi Baima, and Agostino Gaglio. "Demonstration of Blood, Aloes, and Myrrh on the Holy Shroud with Immunofluorescence Techniques." *Shroud Spectrum International* (December 1984): 3–8.

Brown, Raymond. *The Gospel According to John.* New York: Doubleday and Co., Inc., 1970.

Brown, Raymond E. *The Community of the Beloved Disciple.* New York: Paulist Press, 1979.

Brown, Raymond E. *The Virginal Conception and Bodily Resurrection of Jesus.* New York: Paulist Press, 1973.

Bucklin, Robert. "The Shroud of Turin: A Pathologist's Viewpoint." *Legal Medicine Annual,* 1981.

Damon, P E., D.J. Donahue, B.H. Gore, A.L. Hatheway, A.J. Jull, T. W. Linick, P.J. Sercel, L.J. Toolin, C.R. Bronk, E.T. Hall, et. al. "Radiocarbon

Dating of the Shroud of Turin." *Nature,* vol. 337 (February 16, 1989): 611–615.

Daniel. The ArtScroll Tanach Series. Brooklyn, New York: Mesorah Publications, Ltd., 1980.

Danin, Avinoam, A. Whanger, U. Baruch, and M. Whanger. "Flora of the Shroud of Turin." Missouri Botanical Garden Press, 1999.

Davidsohn, Clara and Minnie Well. *Todd-Sanford Clinical Diagnosis by Laboratory Methods.* Philadelphia: W. B. Saunders Co., 1962.

Frei, Max. "Nine Years of Palinological Studies on the Shroud." *Shroud Spectrum International.* Nashville, Indiana: Indiana Center for Shroud Studies (June 1982): 3–7. (English spelling is Palynological.)

Ganzfried, Solomon. *Code of Jewish Law (Kitzur Shulchan Aruch).* Translated by Hyman E. Goldin. New York: Hebrew Publishing Co., 1963.

Gibbon, Edward. *The Decline and Fall of the Roman Empire.* Volume II. Chicago: Encyclopedia Britannica, Inc., 1952.

Gilbert, Roger, and Marion Gilbert. "Ultraviolet-Visible Reflectance and Fluorescence Spectra of the Shroud of Turin." *Applied Optics* (June 15, 1980): 1930–1936.

Gove, H.E. "Dating the Turin Shroud—An Assessment." *Radiocarbon,* vol. 32, no. 1 (1990): 87–92.

Gove, H.E. "Progress in Radiocarbon Dating the Shroud of Turin." *Radiocarbon,* vol. 31, no. 3 (1989): 965–969.

Habermas, Gary R. *The Historical Jesus.* Joplin, Missouri: College Press Publishing Co., 1982.

Harbottle, German, and Walden Heino. "Carbon Dating the Shroud of Turin," *Archaeological Chemistry-IV:* R. O. Allen, ed., ACS Advances in Chemistry, no. 220 (1989): 313–320.

Hawking, Stephen. *A Brief History of Time.* New York: Bantam Books, 1998.

Heller, John and Alan Adler. "Blood on the Shroud of Turin." *Applied Optics* (August 15, 1980): 2742–2744.

Heller, J. and Adler, A. "A Chemical Investigation of the Shroud of Turin." *Canadian Society of Forensic Science Journal,* vol. 14, no. 3 (1981): 81–103.

Israeli Calendar, 1995. Published by the Government Press Office, Jerusalem, Israel. Obtained from the Israeli Consulate, Boston, Massachusetts.

Jackson, John, Eric Jumper, and William Ercoline. "Correlation of Image Intensity on the Turin Shroud with the 3-D Structure of a Human Body Shape." *Applied Optics* (July 15, 1984): 2244–2270.

Jennings, Peter, ed. *Face to Face with the Turin Shroud.* Oxford England: Mowbray and Co., Inc., 1978.

Jerusalem Bible. London: Darton, Longman, and Todd, 1966.

Josephus, Flavius. *The Life and Works of Flavius Josephus.* Translated by William Whiston (1667–1752). "Wars of the Jews," Book II, chapter X. Philadelphia: David McKay Company, (no date).

Jumper, Eric, and Robert Mottern. "Scientific Investigation of the Shroud of Turin." *Applied Optics* (June 15, 1980):1909–1912.

Jumper, Eric, Alan Adler, John Jackson, Samuel Pellicori, John Heller, and James Druzik. "A Comprehensive Examination of the Various Stains and Images on the Shroud of Turin," *Archaeological Chemistry* III, J. Lambert, ed., ACS Advances in Chemistry, no. 205 (1984): 447–476.

Khamor, Levi. *The Revelation of the Son of Man.* Massachusetts: St. Bede's Publications, 1989.

Lamm, Maurice. *The Jewish Way in Death and Mourning.* New York: Jonathan David, Publishers, 1969.

Lavoie, Gilbert R. "The Difference in the Length of the Arms Is an Optical Illusion." *Shroud Spectrum International* (March 1989): 3–7.

Lavoie, Gilbert R., Bonnie B. Lavoie, Vincent Donovan, and John Ballas. "Blood on the Shroud of Turin: Part I." *Shroud Spectrum International* (June 1983): 15–19.

———. "Blood on the Shroud of Turin: Part II." *Shroud Spectrum International* (September 1983): 2–10.

Lavoie, Gilbert R., Bonnie B. Lavoie, and Alan Adler. "Blood on the Shroud of Turin: Part III: The Blood on the Face." *Shroud Spectrum International* (September 1986): 3–6.

Lavoie, Gilbert R., Bonnie B. Lavoie, Daniel Klutstein, and John Regan. "In Accordance with Jewish Burial Custom, The Body of Jesus Was Not Washed." *Shroud Spectrum International* (June 1982): 8–17.

————. "The Body of Jesus Was Not Washed According to the Jewish Burial Custom." *Sindon.* (December 1981): 19–29.

————. "Jesus, the Turin Shroud, and Jewish Burial Customs." *Biblical Archeologist* (Winter 1982): 5–6.

McCrone, W., and C. Skirius. "Light Microscopical Study of the Turin 'Shroud' I." *The Microscope,* vol. 28, no. 3 (1980): 105–113.

McCrone, W. "Light Microscopical Study of the Turin 'Shroud' II." *The Microscope,* vol. 28, no. 4 (1980): 115–128.

————. "Microscopical Study of the Turin 'Shroud' III." *The Microscope,* vol. 29, (1981): 19–38.

————. "The Shroud of Turin: Blood or Artist's Pigment?" *Accounts of Chemical Research,* vol. 23, no. 3 (1990): 77–87.

Miller, Vern, and D. Lynn. "De Lijkwada Van Turijn." *Natuur en Techniek* (February 1981): 102–125.

Miller, Vern, and Samuel Pellicori. "Ultraviolet Fluorescence Photography of the Shroud of Turin." *Journal of Biological Photography,* vol. 49, no. 3 (July 1981): 71–85.

The Mishnah. Translated by Herbert Danby. Oxford: Oxford University Press, 1933.

Morris, R., L. Schwalbe, and J. London. "X-Ray Fluorescence Investigation of the Shroud of Turin." *X-Ray Spectrometry,* vol. 5, no. 2 (1980): 40–47.

Mottern, R.W., R.J. London, and R.A. Morris. "Radiographic Examination of the Shroud of Turin—A Preliminary Report." *Materials Evaluation,* vol. 38, no. 12 (1979): 39–44.

The New Oxford Annotated Bible. New York: Oxford University Press, 1991.

Orna, Mary Virginia. "Doing Chemistry at the Art/Archaeology Interface." *Journal of Chemical Education,* vol. 74, no. 4 (April 1997): 373–376.

Pellicori, Samuel. "Spectral Properties of the Shroud of Turin." *Applied Optics* (June 15, 1980): 1913–1920.

Pellicori, Samuel, and R. Chandos. "Portable Unit Permits UV/Vis Study of Shroud." *Industrial Research and Development* (February 1981): 186–189.

Pellicori, Samuel, and Mark Evans. "The Shroud of Turin through the Microscope." *Archeology* (January-February 1981): 32–42.

Schönborn, O.P., Christoph. *God's Human Face.* San Francisco: Ignatius Press, 1994.

Schnackenburg, Rudolf. *The Gospel According to John.* New York: Crossroad, 1975.

Schwalbe, L.A., and R.N. Rogers. "Physics and Chemistry of the Shroud of Turin: A Summary of the 1978 Investigation." *Analytica Chimica Acta,* vol. 135 (1982): 3–49.

Whanger, Alan, and Mary Whanger. *The Shroud of Turin.* Franklin, Tennessee: Providence House Publishers, 1998.

Wilson, Ian. *The Shroud of Turin.* New York: Doubleday and Co., Inc., 1978.

Wilson, Ian. *The Blood and the Shroud.* New York: Touchstone, 1998.

About the Author

Gilbert R. Lavoie, M.D. received his medical degree from the Medical College of Virginia and later received a Master's in Public Health from Johns Hopkins School of Hygiene and Public Health. He is board certified in both Occupational Medicine and Internal Medicine. His varied background includes Chief of Epidemiology of the European Command while in the Army, Consultant to the World Health Organization Smallpox Eradication Program in Bangladesh, and he organized and managed a large internal medicine practice in Boston, Massachusetts.

Dr. Lavoie has been interested in the shroud for over twenty years, studying the shroud since he first saw it in Turin, Italy, in 1978. He has authored many original studies on the shroud and has presented these at international conferences around the world. He lives in Boston with his wife, and he has three adult children.

Special Thanks

I am very fortunate to have had each specialized area of my work reviewed or endorsed by experts in their own field of research. I very much appreciate the efforts of the following: Dorothy Crispino, editor and historian who reviewed the history section of Chapter Three; Alan Adler, Ph.D., chemistry professor who reviewed the science section of Chapter Three; Jacob Neusner, professor and rabbinical scholar who previously endorsed Chapter Four in *Unlocking the Secrets of the Shroud*, on the burial rites of Judaism; Stephen Camer, M.D., surgeon, who has reviewed the blood studies of Chapters Five, Six, and Seven; and Peter Schumacher, image processing and remote sensing specialist, who participated in the building of VP8 image analyzers, some of which have been used to evaluate the shroud image. He taught me some very important subtleties about the shroud image and later reviewed and helped to edit Chapters Seven and Eight of this new edition. I also want to thank Walter Abbott, S.J., theologian who reviewed the biblical contents of Chapter Nine. I would like to mention a special thanks to Patrick H. Byrne, Ph.D., who kept me straight on my terminology regarding time and space.

I also want to thank Jack Ballas, engineer; Anthony Opisso, M.D., scriptural and rabbinical scholar; Joyce Farrell, my agent; Vernon Miller, scientific photographer; Reverend Frank

Brinkmann, C.Ss.R. and Jan S. van den Bosch of Dutch Television for their efforts and continued support in this work. I want to thank my family for their patience and support. I am grateful to my publisher John Sprague for his continued interest in this project. Most of all, I want to express my thanks to my editor Debra Hampton who has worked diligently to make this new edition a reality.